A Better Way to Make a Living...and a Life

Thriving in the New World of Work

Peter Bourke

Praise for *A Better Way to Make a Living...and a Life:*

—ɯɯ—

- "*A Better Way to Make a Living...and a Life* is engaging, practical and a reliable help for those looking for exactly that. Read Peter's book and map your path to the career and life God designed for you."

  Chuck Bentley, CEO, Crown Financial Ministries

- "God has called Peter Bourke to serve men and women in their career investment and walk with Christ. He is especially gifted and experienced in the integration of personal intimacy with God and professional excellence for God. It is during uncertain times we all hunger for clarity from the Lord to make sure we are laboring in His best space. Peter, by God's grace has given a blue print for life and living that is inspired and under girded by principles that have stood the test of time, so jump in and enjoy the ride!"

  Boyd Bailey, CEO, Ministry Ventures

- "If you wonder if there is a better way to make a living than what you are doing now, read this book. Peter Bourke understands and communicates about

work, life and fulfillment unlike anyone else in three levels...
  o Personally experienced this miraculous realization and transition himself
  o Professionally "gets it" having been President of a $350 million global HR Organization
  o Passionately ministers to hundreds of people in career transition through his church
Really worth the reading!"

> Brian Ray, Founder, Crossroads Career®
> Network
> www.CrossroadsCareer.org

- Peter brings clarity to the sphere of work in the life of the Christian. The result is a light in what has been sometimes murky confusion between the often competing needs of making a living while at the same time utilizing our gifts and talents and fulfilling God's calling on our lives. This is must-reading for the person who wants to stand on a firm foundation of faith, balance life's important priorities, and also succeed in his or her chosen profession.

> Thomas Mason, Former Executive Vice-President, Focus on the Family

- Peter Bourke has taken the complexity out of exploring a critical life issue. His insights provide a very practical guide to discovering God's purpose and specific plan for our work – "A Better Way to Make a Living" As we help bridge the gap between the church and the workforce, HisChurchatWork.org will be using this resource to help thousands glorify God through their work life. If you're intent on bringing joy and relevance to your work, I challenge you, walk this creative path that Peter helps us navigate. Excellent!

> Doug Spada, Founder and CEO,
> HisChurchatWork.org

- Peter's book will give you an MBA in the field of work and employment. I've read books on finding purpose in your work, finding work to fit your purpose, and everything in between. *A Better Way to Make a Living...and a Life* goes deeper than *What Color is your Parachute* and provides a much broader perspective. It may well become the new "standard" for those trying to make sense of their work life".

  Regi Campbell, entrepreneur and author of *About My Fathers Business* and *Mentor Like Jesus*

- "Work today is a dominant part of our lives and this book will profoundly help readers to put work in its proper perspective... God's!"

  Ron Blue, President, Kingdom Advisors

Contents

—m—

Section III
The <u>Maps</u>: Flourishing in the New World of Work 159

Section IV
The <u>Journey</u>: Stand at the Crossroads and Look...........233

This book is dedicated, with love, to
Devonie, Kelly, Trey, Katie, and Dana.
May God bless each of you to find peace
in Him through your work and lives

Introduction

—m—

I most worry about the people who wake up every Monday morning (after a sleepless Sunday night, of course) wondering why they're doing work that doesn't interest them, that seems to have no useful purpose to them, and, worse yet, seems to be their only option. It's just this person whom I pray this book will serve. There's hope for better alternatives.

Have you struggled with the same issues about work that I have?

- "Why does work dominate my life?"
- "How can I find a better balance between work and family?"
- "Why can't I do work that I enjoy and feel better suited to do?"
- "I'd work for half the pay if I could work half as hard!"
- "Why are there so many corporate layoffs? Will I be next?"
- "What ever happened to career stability?"
- "Is this what God intended when He conceived work?"

There are an enormous number of people who are preoccupied with questions like these—people unhappy with their careers, frustrated by the lack of balance between work and leisure, and frightened by the prospect of running a virtual treadmill until they retire, whenever that might be. Oh, and the "good" news? We'll all live longer because of gains in medical science and will therefore have to work longer to pay for the spiraling costs of health care and senior living. Why? Because Social Security benefits and our 401K accounts probably won't cover our costs of living. Anyone excited about the future yet?

I've had the opportunity over nearly three decades to work with, work for, and manage thousands of people. Having witnessed up close the heart and struggles of the average worker, it's easy to conclude that:

- Few workers are really excited about their work. More often than not, we work to make a paycheck because we have to pay our bills. Most see work as a necessary evil—a life sentence of sorts. When it doesn't seem purposeful, it's drudgery.
- Most are intimidated (some even paralyzed) by the prospect of changing their current work situation. We're filled with doubts: Could I even find a better job? How long will it take? What if I end up worse off, not better? As a result, we tend to stay right where we are, as miserable as that may be.
- Those who go through a stage of involuntary unemployment find it one of the most difficult periods of their lives. It shakes our confidence, rattles our relationships, and, at a minimum, reduces our bank account balances. Therefore, we tend to be frightened by the prospect of unemployment.
- On the other hand, nearly every time I've met someone who has been through a career transition, whether

voluntary or involuntary, they typically exclaim how happy they are. For most, it's one of the best things that ever happened to them because it forced them to make a change, usually for the better.

- Most workers tend to mentally separate work from "life," which is pretty scary for an activity that we spend 70 percent of our lives doing. Often it's because they don't see the purpose of work in the broader scheme of things—other than paying the bills, of course.

- In terms of boundaries, however, work is becoming less and less separated from life. Technology keeps us tethered to our job responsibilities 24/7 and encroaches on our not-so-free time.

- Work can also be the dominant force in the lives of many—and a major source of our pride. We cherish our title, our office, even our business card. In fact, many people work hard, even excessively, because work is their primary source of affirmation. It's where we hear that we're doing a great job or that the company couldn't survive without us.

- And for many, Sunday night is the most restless night of the week. In fact, most heart attacks occur late Sunday evening or early Monday morning. Anyone suppose that's purely coincidental?

I can relate to these issues firsthand, having worked for 28 years at some of the most respected corporations in the world. I've always been committed to my work, putting in 60 hours per week and often being guilty of workaholic tendencies. I was fortunate to have expanding responsibility, increasingly important titles, and higher income as I took on new roles. Eventually, I achieved my ultimate career goal: to become president of an organization—a $350-million outsourcing division with more than 8,000 associates. What more could anyone want? Plenty!

Truth be known, I was as restless as anyone. The corporate environment was challenging and often exciting, and rarely did I have a job I didn't enjoy. On the other hand, there always seemed to be a hole in my heart and in my life. I'd often ask:

- Did God really put me on earth just to increase shareholder value? To spend 50-60 percent of my waking hours in work-related pursuits?
- Why can't I spend more time with my family? I had clearly paid my dues, traveling up to four days a week for years. It didn't make sense to continue to spend so much time away from my wife and three quickly growing daughters.
- Why do some people seem truly happy with their work (and life I suppose), while far too many are unhappy with both? Is it their career choice — or something else?
- What job options are there? They seem endless, from the unique to the mundane. How do people find these jobs? How can I? Or *should* I?

My deeply personal interest in answering these questions motivated me to see if others shared my struggle, so I set out on a journey to find out. What I've discovered is that I was far from alone. In fact, it's now obvious that millions of people regularly wrestle with similar questions about their own career and future, particularly in light of today's changing employment dynamics. That's who this book is for.

This is not a "job search" book. Rather, its goal is to enable Christian workers to find peace in their work and in their life because this elusive notion of being peaceful is multi-dimensional - connected to our faith, our finances, our priorities, and even our relationships. We'll explore these and more in the pages that follow. Today's reality is that the relationship between employer and employee has changed drastically and forever. What about your current employment:

- Are you and others asked to do more work with less people?
- Is your job a candidate to be outsourced? Before you answer too quickly, remember that even drive-up-window cashiers at several McDonald's fast food locations have been outsourced to a virtual agent in India.
- Have you seen layoffs happen more frequently? Corporations now "prune" (lay off) employees as often as practical. And they can do so without worrying about excessive severance payments or the threat of lawsuits claiming unfair labor practices. Layoffs are no longer occasional as they were in the past. Now, they're commonplace.
- What about non-traditional worker relationships— part-time, telecommuting, contract and temporary labor, and job-sharing, among others? They've all grown dramatically in most organizations.

These changing dynamics are downright intimidating for the average American worker, who has to be asking, "Am I next?" "Should I be looking for alternatives?" "How can I minimize my risk in this new environment?"

At the same time, younger workers wonder where they're going with their career and how they can get started in the right direction. Older people question whether they're still employable and if they can compete effectively in the future. Women often ponder the feasibility of restarting a career after raising children. All are valid questions that working Americans should be asking themselves because of these dramatic shifts in the job environment. And while these changes can seem intimidating, they also bring with them some significant opportunities, as we'll see later.

We've all met people who have flourished in their career despite disconcerting changes in the work environment. That doesn't necessarily mean they have a high-powered job or an impressive title and salary. In fact, have you ever noticed that there's almost no correlation between a person's level of happiness and his or her job title or salary? I'm often struck by the satisfaction that workers with modest roles and income generally possess in their work and in life.

What is the key ingredient to finding satisfaction and peace in our work and our life? What is it, in spite of daunting change, that allows certain people not only to survive but to be happy and fulfilled? What role does a person's faith play in this? Is it a matter of knowing their calling? Why do some balance work and life well, while others never will? Where should work fit in the overall scheme of life? These are the questions, among others, that I've set out to answer in this book.

A Better Way to Make a Living ... and a Life

For many, finding a better way to make a living is not necessarily about finding a new job. It *may* be, but often it isn't. It's about knowing where you are in your journey and where you're intending to go. Look at how we plan a vacation, for example. There's a fairly predictable set of steps in the process:

- Why are we going? (What's the purpose? Rest and relaxation? Adventure?)
- Where are we going? (What's our direction or destination? North? South? Warm? Cold?)
- How will we get there? (Air? Car? Train?)

- What else should we consider? (What should we bring? How do we decide what to do?)
- How do we capture/document the journey? (Journal? Pictures? Video?)
- What adjustments do we need to make based on what we encounter along the way?

Sound familiar? Some of us may skip some steps, and others are more methodical, but this is how most of us tend to approach a journey.

When it comes to our career—and life itself—the same planning and preparation is important. Though the specific steps are somewhat different, there are many similarities.

If you're one of the 75 million workers in this country who are self-professed "miserable" in their work – there's hope! God's design is for us to do work that is purposeful and fulfilling – perhaps even in your current job. This book will take you on a journey of sorts—think of it as a "road trip" to finding work that reflects not only your God-given talents but also helps to shape your perspective on your work. Here's the roadmap we'll be using:

Section 1: The Landscape: Today's Work Realities

In the first part of the book, we'll focus briefly on the world of work today and the implications for each of us. We'll see how drastically the rules have changed between employers and employees and we'll uncover the impact of other relevant trends like outsourcing and major advances in technology. You'll find that far too many workers are dissatisfied with their work and we'll explore some of the many emerging career opportunities for those who know how to capitalize on them. Think of this section as the environmental landscape of your journey. Understanding the landscape— both the dangers and the opportunities—is essential.

Section 2: The Context: A Better Way to Make a Living ... and a Life

In chapters 4-7 we'll outline the steps required to successfully navigate this journey. We'll explore the importance of identifying your purpose as a starting point and then aim to find your passion and calling. Ultimately though, none of us can navigate this trip without considering our priorities and the challenge of trying to balance them while keeping our sanity in a fast-paced world. This is among the greatest struggles for most workers. It's why so many of us feel like our life is out of control and unmanageable. It's why our work often feels purposeless and unfulfilling. It's also why many of us don't have a sense of God's peace in our life. We'll unpack these challenges to find answers based on what others have already learned.

Section 3: The <u>Maps</u>: Flourishing in the New World of Work

This section provides the tools and perspectives that are critical to finding a better way. How do you navigate? What do you have to watch out for? Are there different issues for those in the early years of their career and those at mid-career? What about 50+ year-old workers? We'll challenge your paradigms about what it means to be an employee and encourage you to give yourself the flexibility (and motivation) to explore opportunities you may not have considered yet. In essence, we'll look at the keys you'll need in order to thrive in this ever-changing work environment.

Section 4: The <u>Journey</u>: Stand at the Crossroads and Look...

The last section will define the specific steps necessary for your successful journey and encourage you to plan your path and persist in reaching your intended destination— to ultimately experience the peace that God promises to those who follow His steps in our work and lives. In the final chapter we'll uncover the key elements that can enable all of us to experience this peace:

- Your knowledge of and relationship with Jesus Christ
- Your ability to be content
- Your "margin" in your life
- Your relationships — marriage, family, and friendships
- Your use of your God-given talents — purposefully

Is it possible to survive and even succeed in today's work environment without this roadmap? Sure. But with the employment dynamics today, why wouldn't you begin to think far more proactively about your career - both the risks and the opportunities? This book is focused on helping you not only understand these dynamics but, more importantly, learn to approach your career in the context of the bigger, more profound context of your life purpose, your passions, your calling, and your priorities as a Christian.

Section I

The <u>Landscape:</u> Today's Work Realities

—ᛞ—

The first part of this journey requires us to look at the realities of today's work environment. What's different now, and why? How have our jobs changed? How has the unspoken employer/employee contract been revised? What's the state of today's worker? How is the American workforce adapting to the change—or is it? What are the implications for our future? Are career opportunities plentiful? Let's explore these and many other questions.

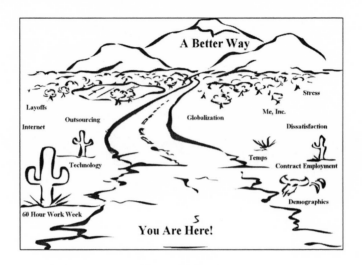

The <u>Landscape</u>

Chapter 1

There's a New Normal

—ᴡᴧᴧᴧ—

There's no doubt that the world of work is changing, and those changes impact all of us. On one hand, employers will need to understand these key dynamics in order to attract, develop, and retain the best talent. It's equally important, however, for workers to understand and embrace these trends. If we proactively take advantage of the opportunities, we won't be victimized by the threats they represent. These changes aren't inherently bad for anyone. I'd even argue that they're beneficial to most—*if* we take advantage of them. Let's look at some of the most significant and obvious trends.

The employer/employee contract

The nature of business itself has changed in the past two decades. As Daniel Pink wrote in his book, *Free Agent Nation*, "For good or ill, the loyalty-for-security bargain that nearly defined the American workforce for several generations is gone."[1] The United States was once characterized by large corporations that offered a promise of lifetime employment, full health benefits, and a modest but reasonable pension that would last until your death and even continue to provide for your spouse. This unwritten "contract" was built on loyalty and went in both directions—employers would do everything possible to protect and retain their employees in difficult financial and economic cycles, and employees would, in most cases, strive to stay with a company as long as possible.

Two things have drastically changed this contract. For the corporation, the motivation for profit has grown more intense, particularly for publicly traded companies, which are measured and rewarded by their ability to grow profitability every quarter. Reducing costs is the surest way to meet this objective in a pinch, and RIF's (Reduction in Force - i.e. layoffs) are the fastest and most predictable way to do that. In addition, employment laws have been relaxed to make the threat of lawsuits for wrongful termination far less daunting for the employer. For the worker— we have become a nation of more capable, better educated, and in many cases more specialized workers. We thrive on challenges, we cherish opportunities to grow and learn, and most of us are not content to stay with one company and hope that we'll be well cared for indefinitely. We want to make our own path and be accountable for our own success. In essence, we are ready, willing, and able to explore new opportunities.

~ Employer/Employee loyalty has been redefined forever ~

There's plenty of evidence that this employer/employee contract has changed dramatically. More than three million jobs have been lost to layoffs since the beginning of 2000. And the mix of unemployed people seems to have changed with significantly more managers and specialty workers (non-blue-collar) than previous generations. That means corporations are finding ways to run their business with fewer people, including fewer white-collar professionals and managers.

One reason for the changing contract between employer and employee is that healthcare and benefits coverage has become one of the largest and fastest growing costs for American corporations. We're living longer and spending more dollars to stay healthy. As costs have spiraled upward, more corporations have shared these increases with their employees, partly to encourage them to make more prudent choices—you'll run to the doctor less often if you have to pay part of the cost, for example—but also because these companies can no longer afford to bear the costs alone. Witness the recent labor union agreements between the United Auto Workers (UAW) and GM and Chrysler that shifts the responsibility for healthcare costs to the UAW, along with billions of dollars to fund the programs. It's a safe bet that companies, large and small, will continue (likely with the government's help) to shift the responsibility for healthcare and related benefits to the individual. In the near future, your health and welfare benefits probably won't be tied to your employer at all, just as 401K pension accounts have become personally owned, managed and portable.

The employer/employee relationship has also changed because we live in a 24/7 culture. Due to the expectations inherent in many companies, employees will do whatever's necessary to fulfill their responsibilities—even if it requires evening or weekend follow-up to do so. This trend is even more challenging today for the average worker, who is "enabled" by new, 24/7 technologies including Blackberrys, high-speed Internet at home, and wireless email access at nearly every hotel and coffee shop in the country.

Me, Inc.

Perhaps the biggest change in the new world of work has to do with the worker's attitude. For decades in this country, particularly during the industrial revolution, a worker's identity—including pride, pension, and future—was closely associated with an employer.

As the last two-plus decades have unfolded, workers have realized that it isn't always prudent to be entirely reliant on just one employer. Perhaps the organization most worthy of our long-term commitment is one called Me, Inc. It requires a different paradigm. It calls on each of us to be largely accountable for our personal career success, our next promotion, our next position, and our own personal development.

At first glance, this may come across as a self-centered approach, a philosophy of "looking out for number one." That's not at all what I'm recommending. I simply mean that we can no longer see ourselves as a ward of the company and blindly give it a lifelong or perhaps even a long-term commitment. Most employers actually prefer not to operate on those terms anymore. They have willingly said, "We'll deal with you on our terms and we expect you to deal with us on your terms." When those terms overlap, it's a good relationship. When they don't, there's nothing wrong with mutually ending that relationship. That's not "me-centered." It's good stewardship of your skills and talents in a culture that focuses on efficiency.

Me, Inc. may seem subtle, but it's the difference between feeling as though you're an employee of XYZ Company compared to seeing yourself as your own entity who's providing valuable services to XYZ —and potentially other employers, even simultaneously—for as long as it suits both your needs and their requirements. With this paradigm shift, there's no confusion about who's responsible for your career and your future. You are! Accordingly, you'll take a personal and intense interest in your skills development, your assignments, and your compensation. More on Me, Inc. in chapter 8.

Workforce demographics

The overall, long term outlook for the average American worker is nothing short of promising, largely because of baby-boom generation demographics. The labor force in this country has grown modestly on an annual basis and will continue to grow slowly—17 million new workers in this decade, for example. Meanwhile, our economy is projected to generate 22 million new jobs in this same period.[2] That's a gap of five million workers, considering the impact of the Baby Boomers' upcoming retirement wave (the first Boomers turned 62 in 2008). This, along with other dynamics, will create a labor shortage and an unprecedented demand for the most qualified talent.

It's also clear that our workforce is becoming more diverse in terms of age, race, ethnicity, and gender. For all categories, this labor shortage represents a tremendous opportunity for workers whose qualifications match the needs of the employer market.

The skill/knowledge and income gap

Will the available workers be equipped to fill these open jobs? Maybe not. Of the 22 million new jobs generated by our economy this decade, 60 percent will require skills that only 20 percent of our workforce now possesses. Or, seen from another angle, only 26 percent of American workers will have a college degree by the time they turn 30 (nearly 60 percent of whom will be female). We are increasingly a knowledge-based economy whose opportunities are dependent on well-educated and skilled workers. The manufacturing and assembly jobs are increasingly, in many cases, being outsourced or "offshored" to other countries where labor is more available and affordable. The imperative for workers in this country is obvious: a lifetime commitment to training and personal development. Specifically, those skilled in abstract reasoning, problem-solving, communications, and collaboration will be the most employable workers in the new world of work.

~ A college degree = a 76% pay premium, on average ~

Not surprisingly, workers with these skills are able to command higher pay. In 2001, for example, the wage premium for a college degree compared with a high school diploma was 76 percent. That's the difference between making $46,000 (with a degree) and $26,000 (without one) annually.

An economy in transition

The United States has shed five million manufacturing jobs in the last three decades during a generally healthy growth period, both because of productivity improvements and because of the trend toward outsourcing to lower cost labor (often in the Far East). And it's not a pure case of manufacturing jobs going away either. In many cases, the jobs have simply shifted to people with math and computer skills who can run sophisticated, automated manufacturing control systems. The implications for many blue-collar workers are obvious: without skills training, the threat to their jobs is real and profound.

Flexible arrangements—temporary, permanent, contract, and job-sharing

Interestingly, both employers and employees are driving this trend. Employers like the variable nature of these alternative work models (and the associated cost savings), and employees like the flexibility they provide to balance their work and life commitments. They also allow many of us to pursue more than one employer relationship simultaneously.

Twenty years ago in the mid '80s, there were about 600,000 temporary employees in the United States. Now there are between 3 and 5.5 million (if you include contract, contingent, and "on call" employees). More broadly, an estimated one in four working Americans is cobbling together a living outside the bounds of traditional employment, either through contract work, part-time jobs, temp assignments, or some combination of the three.[3] That's more than 35 million people! Companies have good and logical reasons to use these alternatives, not the least of which is the flexibility it gives them to ramp up and ramp down as business conditions warrant.

Flexibility may yet be taken to a whole new level. Societal views on primary wage-earner and caregiver roles, as well as on retirement, are changing—and they may take the 40 hour work week with them. Up to now, the standard work week has been 40 hours. Perhaps 20-hour job descriptions could become the norm. We could then choose one, two, or even three of these jobs, depending on our personal and financial goals.

Outsourcing

The outsourcing and off-shoring (work performed beyond the borders of the U.S.) of many corporate functions—including customer service, technology, manufacturing, administration, and human resources, among others—is projected to grow at a 15 percent or greater compound annual growth rate for the foreseeable future. This trajectory will continue to change the nature of the relationships between companies and employees at every level.

Common wisdom once held that outsourcing was a threat mostly to blue-collar employees. After all, most of what had been outsourced between the 1970s and the mid-'90s was manufacturing and assembly related. Not any more. Name-brand companies like GE and American Express are leading the charge to outsource many of their white-collar job functions like accounting, legal, and even medical positions. The numbers are startling: more than three million jobs were transferred overseas from 1994 to 2000;[4] as many as 14 million more, from all levels of the career ladder, may be moved off shore in the next 10-15 years.[5] That represents nearly 10 percent of the current U.S. workforce.

One example of a recent labor outsourcing trend is medical travel. Consumers visit other countries for everything from facelifts to major surgery. Procedures are often so much less expensive abroad that the consumer saves enough for airfare, lodging, and even sightseeing while there. This category of outsourcing is called person-to-person (P2P) offshoring and is likely to grow to include online tutoring for students, web and software development, and writing and translation services.

Even more compelling is the fact that in the next few years, India's and China's focus on training their massive populations with marketable skills will produce nearly 50 million workers prepared to do what American workers have traditionally done, and often at a fraction of the cost. Thomas Freidman in his best-selling book, *The World is Flat*, recounts this domestic homily on his advice to his teenage daughters: "Girls, when I was growing up, my parents used to say to me, 'Tom, finish your dinner-people in China and India are starving.' My advice to you is: Girls, finish your homework — people in China and India are starving for your jobs."

Outsourcing is here to stay, and Americans in all job classes must prepare for the implications. The facts are obvious — many "electronic" service-based jobs will move offshore while "personal" service jobs won't. It's all about being prepared for the right job.

Globalization

Our workforce is also impacted by increasing globalization—the trade of products and services across national borders. Two decades ago, about 10 percent of our economy came from imports and exports. By 2000, the percentage had risen to 25. Advances in technology, distribution, and communications have made the physical location of the workforce much less relevant than before.

Many are concerned that this trend has a negative overall impact on our economy and the job market. In reality, global trade often *generates* new jobs for U.S. workers. In 1999, for example, nearly 12 million American jobs were supported either directly or indirectly by exporting goods and services (i.e., other companies and countries outsourcing their jobs to American workers). The media often doesn't highlight these facts.

Growth of small businesses

The growth of small businesses—those with fewer than 100 employees—impacts our workforce as well. Today, 99 percent of all businesses in the U.S. are small businesses and they employ more than half of the American workforce. They are also responsible for creating two-thirds of our new jobs in most recent years. That should make those who have never looked for work beyond Fortune 1000 companies stop and think. They may be missing great opportunities within smaller businesses.

Technology improvements

We may curse technology for a variety of reasons, but Bill Gates, Steve Jobs and friends have been instrumental in enabling all of us, both personally and professionally. For example, telecommuting is so commonplace that 28 million workers telecommute today.[6] We can now search for our next job electronically from the comfort of our own desk, and we now have access to our computer and emails 24/7—from anywhere. (Did I mention that there's good *and* bad in most of these trends?)

All of this allows us to accomplish more, serve our customers better, sell to more prospects, and even check the box scores during baseball season while you're in a meeting. The employer certainly benefits in many ways, but the danger lies in the encroachment on our personal lives and our sense of balance. It wasn't very long ago that the average worker could leave his or her work at the office and know it would be there the next day. Now many of us have our work with us all day, every day. Work will never be the same!

Productivity improvements

Technology advancements and productivity improvements also impact this country's labor requirements— either by requiring fewer new workers to support growth or by eliminating the need for current employees through streamlined systems and processes. Productivity is clearly increasing. In 1978, for example, General Motors manufactured five million cars with 454,000 employees. In 2004, it manufactured about the same number of cars with only 118,000 employees, thanks to technology and manufacturing improvements. We're doing much more work with much fewer people.This corporate quest for improved productivity is not likely to reverse itself anytime soon because progress translates to greater profit, which translates into a higher stock price—which is usually good for employees and shareholders alike.

Retirement redefined

Though a wave of Baby Boomers will be eligible to retire in the next 20 years, a recent study found that a surprising 34 percent of workers *never* plan to retire. Obviously the entire notion of retirement is taking on new meaning, partly because so many are finding that they can't afford to retire. With the stock market fall from 2000 to 2002 and then again during 2007-08, many potential retirees have been forced to rethink their plans, often extending their working life by five or more years. What's more, many "boomerang" retirees have returned to the workforce following months or even years in retirement, questioning their ability to live comfortably on what they've saved in light of the rising costs of health care and senior living expenses; perhaps, some just became bored with the idea of retirement.

~ Retirement isn't healthy... or biblical ~

So what?

The employment landscape is shifting right under our feet. Sometimes change occurs so close to our noses that we don't see the forest for the trees. Please don't misread this message, however. Though these changes seem drastic and very intimidating, they should *not* cause you to panic. They should compel you instead to begin planning how to best thrive in this evolving work environment. Here are some implications to consider:

- The work you've been doing may not be as available in the future as it has been. What are you doing to develop skills to match the requirements of jobs that will abound in the next decade?
- The concept of career will take on a whole new meaning for most of us, no longer describing tenure with one company but rather a set of experiences with multiple companies that increase a person's marketable skills.
- The changes are not occurring in a linear fashion. Accelerating technology innovations and corporate

earnings pressures create an exponential-change curve.

- Each of us must be proactive in dealing with these changes. You can't afford to simply "wait and see" how things evolve. Actually, you *could* take that approach, but then you'd likely become a victim of the changes. Workers who proactively take charge of their career will have the best opportunities, particularly since the new work environment represents vast career options.
- Changing employment trends should also prompt you to put work and career in the proper perspective. If you expect your work to give you total fulfillment in life, you'll probably be disappointed. This point will become more compelling as we explore our restless workforce in the next chapter.

Chapter 1 Reflection Questions

- How have you seen the nature of the work world change in your own career?
- Which feeling—intimidation or excitement—comes to mind first as you read about these dramatic employment trends? If intimidation, what steps can you take to overcome it?
- Do you view your career opportunities going forward as being better or worse than a few years ago? Why?
- What action steps should you personally consider, given the current employment dynamics: Training? Planning? Financial "safety net" savings? Other?

Chapter 2

Most are Restless

—ɯ—

A friend emailed me this short story, and no one seems to know its author or origin:

> An American businessman struck up a conversation with a fisherman in a small coastal Mexican village. Noticing his fairly small catch, the American asked why he didn't stay out longer and try for a bigger catch. The Mexican said he had enough to support his family's immediate needs.
>
> "What do you do with the rest of your time?" the American asked.
>
> "I sleep late, fish a little, play with my children, take a siesta with my wife, Maria, stroll into the village each evening where I sip wine and play guitar with my amigos. I have a full and busy life, señor."
>
> "I am a Harvard MBA and could help you," said the scoffing American, who proceeded to advise him to buy a bigger boat and eventually a whole fleet, followed by a cannery, and then have enough money to move to a big city to run his expanding business empire.
>
> "What then, señor?"

The American told him he'd be a millionaire.

"Then what, señor?"

"Then you would retire and move to a small coastal fishing village where you would sleep late, fish a little, play with your kids, take a siesta with your wife, stroll to the village in the evenings where you could sip wine and play your guitar with your amigos."

As a society, our improvements in technology and medical science have allowed us to make great progress along many fronts. We have more wealth, better transportation, improved education, and more information. We live longer and are healthier than ever before. Materially, we live in an era of great promise. Why, then, are we so restless as a workforce?

Perhaps it's because we're losing ground on the relational and spiritual sides of the equation. The technology that makes us more efficient has actually resulted in less time for leisure, not more. It's squeezing out our families, our neighbors, our church, and, for too many, our spiritual walk with God.

That's what it was like for my friend Mark Klee (see sidebar at the end of this chapter) when he worked for a major telecommunications company: "I was working 60 to 70 hours per week, rarely home for dinner in the evening, and largely consumed by my work. Even when I was home in the evenings, I ended up in my home office catching up on email and voice mail or preparing for the next day's meetings."

So what has all of this innovation and advancement helped us achieve? Has it made our lives easier? Are we more satisfied with our work or less satisfied?

Overall worker satisfaction – or <u>not</u>!
The majority of roughly 150 million working people in the U.S. fit into one, or more, of the following categories:

- *Misemployed*: These people are gainfully employed, but for a variety of reasons, they're in the wrong job. Very few studies have tried to determine how much of our workforce fits into this category, but my educated (and conservative) guess would be 25 percent—or roughly 35 million workers.
- *Underemployed*: These workers are overqualified for the position they occupy. Their experience and training offer evidence that they previously held positions with more responsibility, greater pay, and a loftier title. No current measures estimate this portion of the working population.
- *Unemployed*: This group results largely from involuntary separation due to layoffs and corporate restructuring ("We have to let you go") and from voluntary separation ("I quit"). Roughly nine million people were unemployed as of late 2008.
- *Dissatisfied*: These workers may be well qualified but are unhappy with their current role, their career prospects, their manager, the work environment, the work requirements, or other aspects of their job. Various employee satisfaction surveys suggest this group ranges widely from 30 to 70 percent of today's workers.

> ~ There are nearly 75 million
> relatively "miserable"
> workers in the U.S. today ~

- *Overworked*: People in this group may like the work they do and even the work environment. The problem is the sheer amount of work that must be accomplished to do the job well. With average hours of work per week on the rise, this is also a large and growing group.

- *Fully and happily employed*: This group is generally satisfied with their current work and their future career prospects. By most estimations, this is considerably less than 50 percent of the U.S. workforce today.[7]

Which of these categories best describes you? More than one? Scary, isn't it?

What's causing the workforce to be so restless? A set of factors has been gaining momentum at a pace we can barely perceive. The challenge and opportunity rests in our ability to deal with the following forces that contribute to worker unrest.

Over-worked and Over-stressed

While a certain amount of stress has always been associated with work, there's little doubt it has become more pronounced in recent years. We feel pressure to work more hours. Our companies set growth goals that often seem unattainable, yet we seem to find ways to achieve these goals. All of that adds up in "wear and tear" – physically and emotionally. The result is stress and overwork, as evidenced by the following:

- The percentage of married workers who live in dual-earner households has increased from 66 percent in 1977 to 78 percent in 2002. Nearly 50 percent of working women say they would take a pay cut if it meant they could spend more time with their kids; the same portion said they'd leave their job if their spouse made enough money for the family to live comfortably.[8]

- The combined work hours for dual-earner couples has risen from 81 hours per week in 1977 to 91 hours in 2002. Effectively, our children have lost 10 hours of Mom and Dad's time per week over this 25 year period.
- A substantial number of us have also had a great deal of our work spill over to our home life through e-mail, voicemail, conference calls, and the like. (So much for today's efficient, time-saving technologies!)
- American workers spend more than $11 billion per year on various methods of coping with stress and these stress-related problems are estimated to cost U.S. industry $300 billion annually.

Even our marriages are negatively impacted by these factors. Work by itself is demanding enough, but when you add together the excessive hours and the travel demands of our many roles, you create a recipe for personal problems—affairs, workaholism, and a family without available and energetic parents to hold things together.

As Richard Swenson outlined in his book, *Margin: Restoring Balance to Busy Lives,* numerous "overloads" contribute to our stressed-out condition, including debt, traffic, information, and noise to name a few. Swenson, a physician who has treated many patients with no margin in life (think about "margin" as the white space in a book) believes all this "progress" creates deeper personal problems:

"Progress has given us unprecedented affluence, education, technology, and entertainment. We have comforts and conveniences other eras could only dream about. Yet somehow, we are not flourishing under the gifts of modernity as one would expect. We have ten times more material abundance than our ancestors, yet we are not ten times more contented

or fulfilled. Margin has been stolen away, and progress was the thief. We must have room to breathe. We
need freedom to think and permission to heal. Our
relationships are being starved to death by velocity.
No one has time to listen, let alone love. Our children
lay wounded on the ground, run over by our high-
speed good intentions."

Does any of this sound familiar to you? Does it describe
some, if not many, of the people you know in the workforce?
In your neighborhood? At church? Maybe even in your own
household?

Job dissatisfaction and employee turnover

Job dissatisfaction often has much to do with a misalign-
ment between the job skills required and the skills of the
person doing the job. It's no wonder...

Ask people you know how they ended up in the career
field they're in today. You'll find that for many, their
"choice" was largely accidental. Most people don't know
what they want to do with their career when they leave high
school or college. They don't even know what their options
are. They're in their line of work because they happened to
know a friend who knew a friend who had a job opening.
Is it any surprise, then, that millions of people don't feel as
though they're doing work that's consistent with their God-
given talents? No wonder so many people feel unfulfilled
and dissatisfied.

Lynn Franco, director of The Conference Board's
Consumer Research Center, has noted that job satisfaction
has been steadily declining since 1995, when it peaked at
nearly 59 percent. "As technology transforms the workplace—accelerating the pace of the activities, increasing
expectations and productivity demands, and blurring the lines
of work and play—working Americans are steadily growing

more unhappy with their jobs."[9] The Conference Board's research suggests that less than 46 percent of workers are satisfied today. Fewer than half of us!

These additional facts further confirm the plight of workers today:

- According to a recent study of 10,000 U.S. workers, 73 percent are receptive to or actively looking for a new job today—and roughly 25 percent of them actually look for new work while they're at work.[10]
- The overall annual job turnover rate for non-government workers in the U.S. is 45.8 percent—nearly half the workforce!
- The average employee stays with his or her employer for 3.5 years and will hold between 13 to 15 jobs in the course of a career. The only industry segment to see an increase in tenure is the government sector at 7.2 years.[11] (Interestingly, the government is one of the few remaining employers that offers a traditional pension/retirement plan.)

Loyalty continues to wane and the significance of these facts on both employees and the employers is profound. For the employee, our health and mental well-being are certainly impacted. We spend the majority of our waking hours in our work, and the burdens we carry at work will affect the other non-working aspects of our lives.

For the employer, numerous studies suggest that a dissatisfied workforce will be less productive and their performance will suffer, whether in selling and serving customers, balancing the books, supporting patients, or anything else.

~ Money doesn't buy happiness - or job satisfaction ~

Chasing the almighty dollar (until it catches you)

For many, money is the scorecard of life. We strive to earn more, only to find that while we continue to acquire more toys, bigger homes, and nicer cars, we're caught on life's economic treadmill. The evidence: We don't save enough, we're declaring bankruptcy at record levels, and we're addicted to debt. In fact, 52 percent of employees (more than half of us!) say they manage their finances by living paycheck to paycheck. Even among people who earn $75,000 or more a year, 34 percent live on the edge.[12] Consumer debt in this country is on the rise, reaching $2.4 trillion in early 2007. The average American credit card holder owns nine credit cards and an average total balance of $4,800. That's not each household, but each card holder! The average new automobile loan in 2002 was nearly $22,000, and the majority of these loans are being financed for more than four years. We're also setting records for going broke; nearly 1 in every 35 households filed for bankruptcy in 2007 and with the recent mortgage woes in this country, that number is likely rising.

Many assume that the way to beat this cycle is to work harder and to make more money ... and then they end up outspending their income again. It's a trap. Wealth and spending do not hold the key to happiness and satisfaction and are certainly not the objective of the spiritual life that God wants us to live. Yet consumerism appears to be an overriding priority in our culture.

A recent Princeton University study shows that higher income plays a relatively small role in people's daily contentment. In fact, one notable finding showed that men making $100,000 per year spend 19.9 percent of their time on passive leisure compared to 34.7 percent for men making $20,000.[13] It reminds me of the Mexican fisherman story at the start of this chapter.

This begs the question then: what *does* make us satisfied in our work and in life? That's what the balance of this book intends to help with. As Russ Crosson concludes in his book *A Life Well Spent*,

We have increased our lifestyles, but in the process haven't we also lost our ability to really live? We have amassed wealth, not wisdom. We have given our children toys, not time...We have been in a rush to run a race without understanding the finish line. Could it be that we are being robbed of our very lives because we are not thinking correctly about why we have money and what we are to do with it?[14]

When work lacks purpose

I contend that if you asked a random group of 10 people who are unhappy in their current work what job would really make them happy and then you could wave a magic wand and granted their wish, a large portion of them would be equally unhappy within a few short months. If that's true – it must not be the job itself in many cases.

Perhaps the most common reason that millions of workers are relatively miserable in their work is that they miss God's purpose and perspective on work. Without it, work can seem aimless and interminable. We work hard, we try to save for the future (often not successfully), and the treadmill never seems to stop (or even slow for that matter)!

On the other hand, if work has purpose beyond helping us pay the monthly bills it can actually be downright meaningful. This may represent the difference between the person who dreads every Monday of a new work week and those that are excited (and grateful) about the tasks and challenges of work – and the personal development and ministry opportunities that our work can provide. It's the difference between work and God being mutually exclusive in our lives (or at least separate) and work and God being integrated (where our work-life is God-filled). Are you integrating the two in your life?

Who *is* satisfied?

In spite of this relatively bleak picture, there are actually many workers today who *are* relatively satisfied with their work. The question: who are they? A *Wall Street Journal* Career Journal survey recently concluded that those who are most satisfied have found work that provides:

- Good intellectual stimulation
- Strong job security
- High level of control and freedom in what they do
- Extensive direct contact with customers/clients

Another study indicates that "prestige" (as defined by the public's perception) associated with a job directly correlates to job satisfaction.[15] It contends that job prestige is spiraling downward for many occupations today; notable examples include accountants and real estate agents. In the U.S., only 1 in 10 people believe these jobs carry great prestige. The most prestigious positions might surprise you:

Occupation	% of the public who view their job as prestigious
Scientists	52 percent
Doctor	52 percent
Firefighter	48 percent
Teacher	48 percent*
Military Officer	47 percent
Nurse	44 percent
Police Officer	40 percent[16]

*[Note for teachers: 30 years ago this number was 29 percent; the overall job satisfaction for teachers has climbed from 40 percent to 57 percent in the same period]

Yet another survey reveals more than four out of five U.S. workers are not currently in their "dream" job. What defines the dream job?

- enjoying the work experience
- applying their talents
- feeling as though they are making an impact
- having fun at work

[Note: Only 12 percent of those polled listed "salary" as a key criterion for a dream job.][17]

Specifically, the following job categories had the highest percentage of workers who felt they have their dream job and you'll notice little correlation between those listed and high income jobs:

- police and firefighters (35 percent)
- teachers (32 percent)
- real estate professionals (28 percent)
- engineers (25 percent)[18]

In reality though, employee satisfaction usually has less to do with prestige and/or having the "dream" job. For the Christian worker it has far more to do with our perspective on our work – and God's perspective on our work. Section two of this book will explore this in depth.

Employees: Wake up!
Given the dynamics above, is it any wonder many working Americans are less than enthralled with their personal and

career situations? The trends suggest that these issues are likely to get worse before they improve.

You'd think that at some point in this vicious cycle we'd say, "Stop the insanity!" and decide to change. Change our spending and savings habits. Change our careers to better align with our priorities and God-given talents. Change our perspective about work and where it properly fits in our life. But most of us don't. In fact, most are unwilling and/or ill-prepared to look at alternative ways to make a living...and a life, for the following reasons:

- *Fear of leaving the security of your current job.* The path of least resistance, and certainly the least amount of toil for the average worker, is to keep doing what you've been doing. There's safety and security in working in an environment to which you've become accustomed, even if you're not happy in the environment. In essence, the easiest thing to do is nothing at all.
- *Lack of confidence in your ability to be successful in another endeavor.* Often people have an interest in a career path but lack the confidence to pursue it, either because they've seen others try and fail or, more likely, they simply doubt their ability to make it happen.
- *Lack of financial resources.* Many others don't think they can afford to take a cut in pay to do work they really want to do and are not prepared to make the sacrifices needed to make the change. Others don't have the capital required to start a new business or buy an existing one, even if they earnestly believe it would be a good fit for their skills and interests.
- *Lack of faith.* Some people have difficulty believing that God wants them to do work consistent with their priorities and talents. They may also lack the faith

that God will provide for their needs as they strive to find work better suited to their skills, experience, passions, and priorities. Our current work becomes the "safety net" as we lack the faith needed to navigate the trapeze of finding a better way.

~ Trust God: pursue the work God designed *you* for...and *for* you ~

For those with the courage and the faith to take action, here are a few suggestions:

- There are few legitimate reasons to be "ok" with being miserable in your current work situation. It's not healthy either physically or mentally, it's usually not rewarding either financially or personally, and it certainly isn't fulfilling. God never intended us to live "quiet lives of desperation" in our work, as Henry Thoreau once said. Instead, he wants us to understand His perspective on our work and His calling on our life.
- Job trends and employment dynamics are in your favor. The more you understand where the opportunities exist, the more likely you are to bravely seek to capitalize on them. We'll cover this in more depth in the following chapter.
- Adopt the philosophy that you're no longer simply an employee of a corporation. Rather, you are the CEO of Me, Inc. You are making a valuable asset (you) available to organizations, large and small, public or private, that can best use and leverage your skills. That may be as a full-time employee, or it may be as a contractor. You're ultimately responsible for the development of this asset, the marketing of this asset,

and the care and feeding of you! (See chapter 8 for more details)

- If you *expect* job permanence and career longevity, don't! You may be the exception to the rule, but it's more prudent to accept that job transition is the "new normal" for the average worker. Look for the next best opportunity to leverage your skills and experience within your current company or another because the best time to find a new job is when you have one—not after you lose one.
- Keep a healthy perspective on your work and where work fits in the scheme of your life here on earth. Yes, it does represent a large part of your time, but it's not intended to dominate your existence—at least not to the exclusion of healthy relationships (like marriage and children, for two notable examples) and your ultimate relationship with Jesus Christ.

In the chapter that follows, we'll shift gears and look at how you can break the chains holding you back from overcoming the obvious challenges and, more importantly, determine how to capitalize on the opportunities presented by these changing employment dynamics.

First though, it must be obvious by now that I have strong opinions about the nature and evolution of the workplace. But you'll learn less from my strong opinions than you will from ordinary people who have made decisions to pursue their passion or to re-prioritize their lives in order to do work that is both fulfilling and suits them well. That's why I've scattered throughout this book the stories of people who have taken the steps and in some cases, made difficult choices to transition into a better way to make a living. Many of these stories were the motivating factors for this book. Their profiles are inspiring, entertaining, and perhaps even personally convicting stories of American workers who have overcome, adapted to, and even benefited from the changing employment environment. I found some striking similarities in their experiences:

- They haven't necessarily become rich, but many have found ways to lower their cost of living to accommodate a career change, and they usually end up making a sufficient income to satisfy their needs.
- They are doing work that leverages their talents and, better yet, their passions. They aren't satisfied to do work they aren't fit to do or can't be happy doing.
- In many cases, they have faithfully followed biblical principles and put God at the center of their lives. They haven't overextended themselves with debt. They've faithfully given to church or charitable causes. And they consistently seem to be able to keep their work in the proper perspective – God's perspective, that is.
- They have also, in most cases, been able to maintain a sense of balance between work and other pursuits, including family, hobbies, and volunteer work.
- Finally, they seem genuinely satisfied in their work, their life, and their future prospects.

The Klee's are a great example of these traits:

~ God has a plan and worry isn't required: Mark and Jamie Klee ~

Mark was an All-American pole vaulter from the University of Arkansas with degrees in geophysics and mechanical engineering from the University of Alabama. That's where he met his wife Jamie, a self-professed tomboy from Mississippi who was one of three women in the undergraduate mechanical engineering program.

Starting his career with Andersen Consulting (now Accenture) in 1989, Mark felt he had found the perfect company for his career aspirations. It was professional, well-respected, and filled with capable people. Jamie applied her talents to a position with the Environmental Protection Agency. She found the agency too bureaucratic and inefficient, but worked there for five years until her second of three children was born. She and Mark hoped his income would allow her to stay home with their kids.

Mark had flourished in his career with Andersen. For the seven years he spent there, he was assigned projects in the Atlanta area, where they had moved when they married in 1990. He worked long hours but traveled only occasionally. Then the reality of life in the consulting industry struck when he was assigned to a full-time project for a client in Houston. It required him to be away from home nearly five days a week. Mark and Jamie were determined to find a better career option.

"I was largely motivated by money at the time," Mark explained, "and I had always wrestled with a desire to have my own business." Accordingly, Mark and Jamie decided to get involved with Amway. Amway offered a great opportunity but required a huge commitment.

"We were pretty miserable. I was working between 70-80 hours per week for two different organizations, we had two children, going on three, and I was assigned to a project in Houston," Mark lamented. They decided change was necessary—on several fronts. While both were brought up in Christian homes, they were never faithful at tithing. Together, they committed to begin giving 10 percent of their income back to God. They also knew that lowering their monthly expenses would provide them more career flexibility, so they downsized from a house on a golf course in an affluent suburb to a more modest house 20 miles away, reducing their mortgage expense by 35 percent.

Mark left Andersen and went to work in the information technology field at a financial institution for a year, and then spent three years with Alltel, a telecommunications company. Although he liked the work, he was working outrageous hours in a high-pressure job, and, according to him, "my family was being severely compromised."

It was Christmas 1998 when job demands nearly caused Mark to miss the Klee's annual trip home to visit family for the holidays. That, combined with a particularly powerful Sunday sermon about giving an account on the Day of Judgment for our lives on earth, resulted in genuine change for Mark and Jamie.

In May 1999, Mark resigned from Alltel with no idea what was next for him and his family. He only knew that he was working too hard, was too preoccupied with making more money, and was compromising his family life. "One thing I remember when I resigned is how often people remarked that they wish they had the guts to do the same."

The Klee family immediately took a vacation to the beach to begin to make up for lost time. Mark bought and read more than 20 books related to the real estate business. "I had always enjoyed construction and working with my hands and thought that while I determined what to do with my career, I could buy a house that needed some work, fix it up, and sell it for a profit."

As good fortune—or rather God's hand—would have it, Mark's previous employer contacted him a few months after he left and invited him to work part time. He agreed to work no more than two days per week, and they paid him just what he needed to cover his recently reduced monthly expenses. That gave him the opportunity to grow his newfound interest in real estate into a business that could support his family long-term.

Mark has developed his real estate business considerably since he began learning the field in 1999. He buys and sells distressed properties, has begun to buy houses and provide lease/purchase options to prospective buyers, and now provides real estate information to other investors via a subscription service on the Internet and training seminars.

"I enjoy the work I do, I'm able to work from home most days, and I set my schedule according to what's important to me and my family," Mark said, marveling at the change. His day also includes more than an hour of quiet time in prayer and reflection each morning. "I am still amazed at the inspiration and peace that my quiet time provides," he said.

The changes the Klee's made also allowed Jamie to home school their children, now ages 14, 12, and 8. "We're together as a family most days, all day," she says. "When I compare that to how we existed a few years ago, I'm still amazed at the change."

Lessons Learned

Mark: "A couple has to come together and decide what's important to them and make choices accordingly. We had priorities in our life, but our choices weren't reflective of those priorities."

Jamie: "Every time we made good, biblical decisions about our work, our finances, or our lives that reflected what God had put on our heart, we have been blessed for those decisions. We trust that God has a plan for our lives and when you have that confidence, worrying isn't required."

Chapter 2 Reflection Questions

- How satisfied are you with your current work?
- Which of the following describe you?
  - o Misemployed
  - o Overworked
  - o Stressed out
  - o Fulfilled and purposeful
- If you're dissatisfied, why? Do you think the issues are primarily related to your perspective? The job's use of your skills and talents? Your work environment? Or something else?
- Have you considered alternative work and/or careers that could be more satisfying and fulfilling? If so, what? If not, do any fears or obstacles stand in your way?

Chapter 3

Opportunities Abound

—ɷ—

An Autobiography in Five Short Chapters
By Portia Nelson

I
I walk down the street.
There is a deep hole in the sidewalk
I fall in.
I am lost... I am helpless.
It isn't my fault.
It takes me forever to find a way out.

II
I walk down the same street.
There is a deep hole in the sidewalk.
I pretend I don't see it.
I fall in again.
I can't believe I am in the same place
but, it isn't my fault.
It still takes a long time to get out.

III
I walk down the same street.
There is a deep hole in the sidewalk.
I see it is there.
I still fall in... it's a habit.
My eyes are open.
I know where I am.
It is my fault.
I get out immediately.

IV
I walk down the same street.
There is a deep hole in the sidewalk.
I walk around it.

V
I walk down another street.

Be encouraged—there's hope! In fact, there's good reason for downright optimism in your career – as long as you don't keep walking down the same "street" as noted in the autobiography above. Let's look at some of the compelling trends that should encourage you about future job opportunities.

A growing economy – at least long term

While home prices and the U.S. economy significantly sputtered in 2008 related to the financial and credit crisis throughout the U.S. (and the world), there are plenty of reasons to feel bullish about career opportunities going forward. According to a recent Bureau of Labor Statistic (BLS) report, the number of employed American workers is anticipated to increase by 22 million to a total of more than 165 million workers by 2012. (As noted in an earlier chapter, only 17 million people will likely be available to fill these new jobs.)

And while the total number of jobs will grow substantially, the nature and mix of these jobs in the coming years is likely to shift. The challenge is to better understand what the trends will be and how we can best adapt to them.

The growth of small and service-oriented businesses

The statistics are overwhelming: More people are figuring out that the job stability previously promised by large corporations is too often an unrealistic expectation. That's why so many people are starting, buying, or working for small businesses. And the future for small businesses looks bright. In fact, they employ more than half of the American workforce. These businesses are also responsible for creating two-thirds of the new jobs in most recent years. Contrary to common belief, the best career opportunities often exist outside of the biggest, most visible corporations.

Though we couldn't possibly outline every conceivable small business opportunity in this book, we can explore some examples that are indicative of these positive trends. Take a small business model that 14 million Americans have already tapped into, for example—direct selling.

~ Your next best career opportunity may be in a small business ~

The direct-selling industry has exploded over the past 20 years. You would recognize the companies in this business by names like Shaklee, Tupperware, The Pampered Chef, Avon (which was started back in 1886), Creative Memories, and Mary Kay, among others. It's now a $30+ billion industry in the U.S., according to the Direct Selling Association. While 14 million Americans are involved in the industry, more than 80 percent of them are female. With the notable exception of Avon, opportunities like this hardly existed a couple of decades ago, yet they now represent nearly 10 percent of the American workforce! What's fueling the growth? The public's insatiable consumerism, efficient distribution mechanisms, and the ability to reach millions of people far more efficiently than could be done previously. Consumers seem more than willing to spend money on their looks, pets, children, entertainment, cars, and their homes. As evidence, here's a look at how the Association estimates the $30+ billion was spent as recently as 2005:

- Personal Care (cosmetics, jewelry, etc.) $10B
- Home/family care (cleaning, cookware, etc.) $8B
- Wellness (weight loss, vitamins, etc.) $5.7B
- Services/other (scrapbooking, etc.)$4.5B
- Leisure (books, videos, toys) $1.5B

Consider two other opportunities for the aspiring small business entrepreneur:

- *Franchises of every shape and size.* There are over 3,000 franchise organizations today and a stunning number of locations. Some notable examples (number of franchise locations in parentheses)
  - o Subway (20,000+)
  - o Dunkin' Donuts (5,000+)
  - o Domino's Pizza(4,500+)
  - o 7-11 Stores(4,000+)
- *Small, service-based businesses with relatively little financial capital required.* These include painting, handyman, lawn care, pressure washing, personal computer services, pet sitting services, and myriad others that tend to rely upon your willingness (or skills) to do daily chores and tasks that others would

rather pay someone else to do. And with most you can operate from your home!

Of course, owning and/or operating a small business isn't right for everyone. In fact, many actually fail within the first few years of operation so be prudent in your choices. The right small business for you, if there is one, will depend on many things unique to you, including:

- *Your available capital.* Some businesses require significant capital and may represent too much financial risk for you and your family.
- *Your skills and passions.* Perhaps above all other considerations, if you consider starting or buying a business, make sure the nature of the work and industry is compatible with your skills, passion, interests, and priorities. Hard work alone is often not enough to make a business successful that doesn't suit you.
- *Your entrepreneurial attributes.* A significant investment of time and energy is usually required for people to succeed. There are too many business failures to believe that it's easy. Spend time with or interview others in the business you're considering and ask them about the good, the bad, and the ugly aspects of the business.
- *Your previous experience.* Do you have enough experience in the business you're targeting to give you a high probability of success? If not, can you learn the business? Do you have a partner who brings the requisite skills? Or, can you hire the talent that has the skills?

Regardless of your choice, do enough research to ensure that you've considered all available options and are well aware of the risks and rewards. Those who travel this path usually find it exhilarating and intimidating all at once.

Globalization

Equally compelling is the potential to join a business or create new businesses that capitalize on the ever-growing, global nature of our economy. Americans have a tendency to hold a U.S.-centric view of the world. Countries like Brazil, Russia, India and China represent the world's largest emerging economies and their massive populations are becoming better educated. With this progress, they have better income-producing capabilities and there will be plentiful opportunities to sell products and services (computers, music, cell phones—all are experiencing explosive growth in these developing countries) to a huge new segment of the world's population. There are actually many employers in these countries who are offering employment to U.S. workers who are willing to relocate overseas so that they can tap into our experienced workforce. It may even represent a great mission field opportunity for those who see their work as an opportunity to spread the good news of Jesus' gospel considering the Christian-minority nature of these populations.

The Internet

It's a phenomenon like no other. Who would have thought this emerging technology revolution would become such an integral part of our lives? The Internet is increasingly available, increasingly useful, and fast becoming a significant employment segment. It's also a great example of how shifts in our technology, economy, and culture can represent both threats and opportunities.

~ Have a great product idea?
You can reach millions with
the Internet instantaneously ~

The opportunities certainly exist for those who are tech-savvy. They can work in Internet application development and infrastructure support, or they can take advantage of what the Internet provides. One notable example: more than 1.3 million people around the world earned their primary or secondary income selling products and services on eBay in 2007.[19] To these people, eBay is the world's largest shopping mall and the sellers are the shop owners in the "mall." It's amazing to think that ten years ago a retailer's ability to reach thousands of customers was both difficult and expensive. Today, a retailer or independent service provider can access millions of people globally in a matter of minutes through channels like eBay, Amazon, and MySpace, to name a scant few.

The Internet is the technology that enables those with a clear idea of their passion in life to turn that passion into something that can actually put food on the table. There are literally thousands of other ways for you to leverage this new, huge, and still emerging technology called the Internet. The only limit is your creativity and bravery in pursuing the right opportunities. The Internet is arguably the biggest and most exciting technological innovation of our lifetime. How can you take advantage of it?

New and high-growth job and industry classes
We've already looked at some of the rapidly changing dynamics in today's economy and the employment environment overall. At first blush, these changes can look pretty intimidating—fewer full-time traditional jobs and more frequent layoffs as examples. But there's another way to view these changes: focusing on the emerging high-growth oppor-

65

tunities of the changing work environment and then capitalizing on them. For every threat, there are at least as many new, exciting opportunities. New high-growth industries and job classes represent tremendous opportunities for those alert enough to understand and take advantage of them. Here are a few compelling and encouraging facts about today's "macro" employment dynamics:

Healthcare: The Baby Boom generation is getting older and will live longer than previous generations. This aging population "bubble" will require more medicine, more medical services, more hospital stays, and more home health care. This represents an indisputable opportunity for many who have skills and interests in healthcare. "It's going to be the biggest business of the next three decades," says Gerald Celente of the Trends and Research Institute, which has been predicting workforce trends for more than two decades. Celente believes there will be greater demand for services to care for the needs of Baby Boomers because many are entering their golden years in poor physical condition. Seniors in this country, interestingly enough, are the unhealthiest of all of the industrialized nations in this world. "This immobile society is not aging gracefully," he adds.[20] Nurses, physicians, technicians, radiologists—you name the specialty—are already in high demand, and this demand is expected to continue for the foreseeable future. That creates an opportunity for many to work in a field with relatively competitive compensation and flexible hours (or excessive overtime, if you prefer to maximize your income).

Technology: While there has been a slowdown in technology spending and therefore a slowdown in technology labor requirements to start this decade, few would argue that the U.S. economy is being fueled, in large part, by technological innovations that are allowing for productivity increases, better customer service, and an ability for companies of all sizes to reach more customers more effectively. Even though technology momentum may ebb and flow over time, the future for those who acquire technology skills looks very bright. *Retail:* Like it or not, we're still a consumer-driven society. The media feeds it. Entertainment venues encourage it. And we, the public, buy right into the phenomenon. There's no other explanation for how Wal-Mart can become a $350+ billion-a-year retailer, the country's largest employer (more than 1.5 million employees), and one of the most profitable organizations in the world. All evidence indicates that the public's appetite for more consumer goods and services will continue to grow, which makes the retail industry a healthy employment opportunity—whether working for yourself or for a retail company.

Temporary employment: There are significantly more temporary workers (and often fewer permanent employees) in most organizations today versus a decade ago. The popularity of this employment model for both employer and employee is obvious: it provides flexibility, market-competitive pay rates, and the ability to change (that is, "end") the relationship if the needs of either the individual or the business change. And the concept of temporary employment is not limited to clerical resources, as many believe. A recent breakdown of temp labor by category may surprise you:

•Administrative/clerical support	21 percent of total
•Operators, fabricators, laborers	17 percent
•Professional specialty	16 percent
•Precision, production, craft, and repair	12 percent
•Services	11 percent
•Executive, administrative, managerial	9 percent
•Technicians and related support	7 percent
•Sales	6 percent

Source: U.S. Bureau of Labor statistics

Having spent several years with a staffing company myself, I can confidently project that this trend will continue and will provide many opportunities for millions of American workers in the coming decade—across many functional specialties and at all levels within most organizations, including "temp" executives.

What about a college degree?

Some may argue that a college education is required to take advantage of these trends. For most of us, college was all about growing up and learning how to think. Personally, I'm not sure I learned much in college that I could actually apply when I started my career with IBM in 1981. Though plenty of studies support the fact that those who have a degree earn more money on average than those who don't, a college education is by no means a prerequisite to living a successful, happy, and purposeful life. The key appears to lie more in our ability to develop specialty skills that are in high enough demand to allow us to make a reasonable living. As Proverbs 30:8 says, ...*Give me neither poverty nor riches but give me only my daily bread*. The rest of the equation is all about having a clear view of our purpose, passion, and priorities in life and having a healthy perspective on where work fits within this context.

Surprising job categories

The size of many career fields in the next several years (through 2014) may surprise you. I've outlined in the appendix some "fun facts" about specific Department of Labor employment categories along with notes (and opinions) related to each. This list isn't comprehensive but will give you a sense for the relative size of each. I've also thrown in some categories that aren't very large, but interesting nonetheless. You'll see that there's plenty of variety for the average worker today. The challenge lies in finding the work that best suits you.

Hot new trends

It's always fun to meet people who are savvy enough to see a new trend and then capitalize on it by providing relevant products and services. One example would be video game companies—including the technology designers who build these programs—that have grown out of the trend toward home-based game platforms from Sony, Nintendo, Microsoft, and others. Or, consider the number of jobs that have been created in and around the iPod explosion—carrying devices, speaker systems to blare the music from these tiny platforms, or plugs that allow them to work in our cars or in the shower. You name it, someone has (or will) develop it. None of the companies that make these complementary devices existed until a few years ago. The challenge is to watch for these trends and figure out how to support the market's demand for them. Why not leverage some of these fast developing trends:

- *Home-based PC and wireless networks.* Most of us have no idea how to install, troubleshoot, or support them.
- *EBay.* Many people want to sell their used goods but many have no interest in managing the process, and they need assistance.
- *Anything "green".* Environmentally friendly products, services, and causes are all the rage of late – how can you leverage the practical and political momentum in your next career?.
- *Blackberrys, iPhones, and equivalent devices.* They function as cell phone/camera/e-mail/GPS/video recorders/MP3 players plus whatever else someone can think to add to them.

- *Solar and other non-traditional energy sources.* Why not take advantage of this trend?
- *What else?* Just keep your eyes open because these trends usually represent tremendous career or business opportunities for those who proactively capitalize on them. Every single day people think of great ideas and do nothing with them – what about you?

Unique careers

Some of us are motivated to find the job that few others have ever heard about, much less occupied. If you're interested in a job or career that's a little different than others, there are plenty of web sites to investigate. Some universities have even designed unusual degree programs for those looking for the unusual careers:

- CSI "Any Town" USA? Baylor University in Texas offers courses in forensic archaeology, death scene investigation, and hostage negotiations. Every day of class promises to be dramatic!

~ Do you have a unique career or story? Share it with us at:
www.betterwaytomakealiving.com ~

- Old car need work? McPherson College in Kansas has a four-year degree in automotive restoration technology. SPEED channel recently provided a $100,000 donation to the program.
- Run away to the circus to paint? Ringling School of Art & Design in Florida has the latest technology in hardware and software at your fingertips—and you'll have 60 art galleries, sandy beaches, and baseball spring training camps to keep you entertained in the local area.

- Talent agent? Southwest Missouri State promotes a business management program that prepares you to be an event promoter, personal manager, or talent agent.
- Rock Climbing Expedition Leader? The University of Alaska Southeast's outdoor studies program is a certificate program that teaches self-reliance and understanding of group dynamics, and it fosters the leadership skills that will help you succeed as a wilderness guide or as a leader in any walk of life.

Other unusual career opportunities:

Video game tester—If you spend your free time playing video games, this may be the career for you. You can actually get paid for doing it. Your job, should you accept it: To play the game and find things that don't work or don't make sense. You can verify functionality, performance, and "playability" of the games. Believe it or not, many of these jobs require a college degree (but not all of them). The likely career path is to move from this position to video game developer, which does require a computer science degree.

Baseball statistician—Most major league teams employ someone whose job is to keep track of the important statistics (and mundane ones, for that matter) that a 162-game season can generate.

Golf course marshal—Ride around in a cart, enjoy free greens fees and socialize with golfers who are generally in a good mood (perhaps because they're not working?)—not a bad gig. The pay is moderate, but your "office" can be downright spectacular.

Personal concierge—There are few barriers to begin providing personal services for those who are too busy for every day activities like making reservations, shopping, buying gifts—or just about anything else you can imagine. And there's little doubt that people need the help.

Environmental epidemiologist—If it sounds like an earth doctor, it is . . . sort of. These professionals assess diseases and injuries in the overall population. They may look for outbreaks of a virus in a community or the frequency of skateboard accidents at a certain city park—all with the intent of diagnosing the problem and determining solutions to reduce the public's risk. I'll bet you didn't even know this job existed!

These are a few examples of literally thousands of jobs that are perfectly designed for someone. It's a matter of you finding your ideal fit. And if you can't find it, go and create the job or company that allows you to use your gifts and talents. It takes effort, but it's well worth the effort.

The "so what"

I hope you've concluded that there's no shortage of career opportunities. But these opportunities won't simply fall in your lap. The easiest and most common approach most people take to their career is to do nothing at all, and then we feel like a victim when our employer eventually tells us we're part of the latest round of layoffs.

I suppose this represents a strategy, but I'd argue that it's a lousy strategy. The far better approach is to be proactive. To recognize that change as inevitable. To explore and understand the gifts and talents God has blessed you with, to seek out the opportunities that fit you best, and to keep Christ at the center of your journey. Don't miss the power of His presence in the part of your life that usually involves more time, energy, and relationships than any other - your work.

Yes, the world of work has changed. And yes, many workers in this country are less than satisfied in their current position. But if you embrace the notion that career options are plentiful and then firmly embrace God's own profound view of our work (in the next chapter), we'll be ready to explore ideas intended to motivate you to take action and to proactively pursue a better way to make a living...and a life.

Chapter 3 Reflection Questions:

- In what ways do you think today's emerging work trends are most likely to impact your current job or career? Do you think this impact will be primarily positive or negative?
- What do you see as the best opportunities in this new world of work for your current career? For a career alternative?
- Do you know people in your personal or professional life who have changed careers to capitalize on the emerging trends? What steps can you take to explore what they've learned and seek their advice?
- Are there any unique careers that you've contemplated but never pursued? What has kept you from pursuing them? What obstacles would you need to overcome to pursue them now?

Section II

The <u>Context</u>: A Better Way to Make a Living...and a Life

—∿∿—

Given today's work realities, let's delve more deeply into the context of how we can put work and life in perspective. What's the key to making order out of the chaos? For many, it's changing their paradigm—getting a different perspective on their work and the importance it holds in their life. Because most of us spend more than 40 hours per week in and around our job, we often place work at the pinnacle of our priorities. Our work tends to have a dominant impact on our state of mind and, ultimately, our happiness.

If, on the other hand, we could keep work in the proper perspective we'd likely be more content with the work we have today instead of longing for something new. For instance, have you ever met someone who has an "undesirable" job—maybe a janitor, a tollbooth operator, or a hotel maid—who's not only satisfied but even joyful in their work? And, conversely, have you known someone with a "dream job"—I always think of professional athletes here—who, in spite of all their money and fame, are completely miserable?

There are yet others who view work, regardless of the environment, as an opportunity to glorify God every day. They are less focused on achievement, as our culture defines it, and more focused on serving others and showing others the love of Christ.

What, then, should constitute career "success?" How should it be measured? Here's a perspective provided by Russ Crosson in his book, *A Life Well Spent*:

We are all called to different vocations. We cannot all be doctors, developers, accountants, or lawyers. We also need cooks, letter carriers, police officers, grocers, plumbers, printers, and truck drivers. Therefore, regardless of a person's vocation, only God really knows if he or she is successful. We do not know the degree of someone else's obedience. We can measure his or her wealth and riches, but not his or her success; we are only successful if we are obedient. Is an excellent teacher who makes thirty thousand dollars less successful than a professional athlete who sits on the bench and makes three hundred thousand dollars?

In God's definition, their obedience and the degree to which they have maximized the abilities He has given them are the keys to their success. Their income has nothing to do with it. They both could be failures if they are not doing their best or they disobeyed God in choosing their vocation. Since it is God who gives us the ability to make wealth (see Deuteronomy 8:16-18) and God who designs each of us to perform different functions, then the income we earn cannot possibly be the measurement of success.[21]

Finding a better way to make a living is not a secret. It isn't a mystery. And yet, so many workers today are hesitant to resolve to find a better way to make a living. Why don't they aggressively pursue better alternatives, or at least a different perspective?

If you're convinced that the time for change is now, the next four chapters are for you. They're designed to help you look at the context of work and life—our purpose, our calling, our priorities, the implications of these dimensions on our career and life choices, and the challenge of creating life-balance amongst them. This section is not a primer on finding any old job. Rather, the goal is to help you find the work that God intended for you to have. In fact, the right work for you may very well be the work you already do.

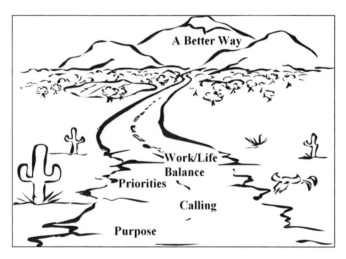

The <u>Context</u>

Chapter 4

Purpose: Work in Its Proper Perspective—God's

—∿∿—

Why do some people seem satisfied with their work, their balance between work and life, and their prospects for the future, when most of us aren't? Is it all about the actual work we do? Or is there more to it?

To find the answer, let's embark on this journey toward a new way of making a living...and a life in the new world of work. The journey begins with our perspective.

Work as our identity

While the Bible discusses work as a good and noble activity to be done dutifully and cheerfully, it doesn't suggest that it should be *the* central part of our lives. Yet many of us make our careers the top priority. Our identity is often wrapped up in our work. We build our pride on it and let it dominate our thoughts.

I am guilty as charged on this front. I've never met a job or a company I didn't like. I've already admitted my "Type A" tendencies and workaholic track record. I've always been proud of the companies I've worked for, the titles I've held, and the size of the organizations I've managed—that is, until

79

a few years ago when I began to ask God simple questions like, "Is this all there is to life? More work?"

The emphatic answer for me was, "No!" God never required me to work 60-hour weeks. That was my doing. He never insisted that I move my family six times in the first nine years of our marriage. He never intended for me to be so fully preoccupied with work that I had little time or energy left for other important priorities. After work and family, I had little or no time for anything else, including truly nurturing and developing my relationship with Jesus Christ.

~ Is your identity in your work...or in Christ? ~

Our culture exacerbate this challenge. Think about when we meet someone for the first time. We invariably ask the same question: "So, what do you do for a living?" Is it any wonder that work holds such a grip on our psyche? If work is going well, all seems well. When work isn't going well, however, our attitude, sense of well-being, and even physical strength are negatively impacted. This is most pronounced when workers lose their job, regardless of the reason.

In the Crossroads Career® Network ministry (www. crossroadscareer.org), we help churches support the needs of both the unemployed and those who are employed but at a crossroads in their career as they look for work that's consistent with their God-given talents—and in a way that helps them strengthen their relationship with Jesus in the process. In my involvement in this ministry over the past five years, it's become obvious that when someone loses their job, perhaps even more so with men, they usually struggle emotionally, lose self-confidence, their marriage is tested, and, obviously, their finances suffer. Their entire equilibrium is upset.

Our work clearly plays a central role in our life, for good and practical reasons. At the same time, though, our work shouldn't take on such enormous proportions. While we have an obvious need to earn an income and pay our bills, work for many of us has become our god. The challenge is to determine how to resist (or overcome) this tendency.

God's purpose for our work and our life

These issues beg a few important questions: What is God's perspective on our work? Is it a necessary evil? A punishment? The center of our existence? How does work fit within the broader issue of our purpose here on earth?

Let's start with the fundamental "purpose" question because without clarity of purpose, everything in our lives tends to be fairly meaningless. Without purpose we make decisions based on what feels good or what's most urgent, perhaps even most fun. In essence, we live in and of the world with all of the world's warts.

On the other hand, when we focus on God's purpose for our lives, all of our work and life decisions are shaped accordingly. This "context" helps determine how we allocate our time, how we establish our priorities, and what relationships we nurture. It changes virtually everything.

I heard a great picture of clarity of purpose recently when I asked a new friend what he did for a living. "I'm a free agent for Christ," he answered. Wow! It was one of the most powerful statements I've ever heard about having a biblical worldview: that regardless of what I'm doing—work, play, charity—I do it all for the purpose of Christ's work and His will.

This focus on purpose is the primary reason I left my last corporate job in 2003. It became obvious that if my purpose in life is to use my God-given gifts to fulfill His will—which I understood to involve writing and speaking on career-related topics and serving those who struggle with career and faith issues—I couldn't do it well while working 50-60 hours per week in a corporate environment. Was I certain about how the bills would get paid as I made the transition? Not entirely. But I did have peace about being in God's will and being obedient to His calling. I've also been able to witness God's provisions as we've walked this purpose-driven journey since then. I only wish I had wrestled with some of these hard questions before getting to mid-career. For many of us, that's when it becomes a crisis issue. We could save ourselves a lot of struggles if we started with clarity in our purpose earlier in life.

Consider the illustration of someone starting a new job. What's the first thing we do when we show up for work— immediately jump in and get consumed with aimless activities? Probably not. When effective people take on a new job or challenge, they ask a series of basic but important questions: What's the goal? Why am I here? What do I need to learn? How can I contribute? What am I expected to accomplish?

Only by asking and answering these questions can we begin to gain clarity on where we belong, how we can best contribute, and how we can ultimately achieve success. Not only that, but the more clarity we have on this issue, the more enjoyable our work will be.

Take golf as another illustration – this game can be agony for me if I lose track of its purpose. When I played golf in high school I was hyper-competitive and focused on getting lower scores. That seemed to be <u>the</u> purpose at the time, and when my scores weren't improving, I became easily frustrated. Now that I have a different perspective on the purpose of this great game—to enjoy the beauty of the surroundings, to enjoy the camaraderie with others, to get some exercise and relieve some stress (except when I'm facing a 200-yard shot over water of course)—I've thoroughly enjoyed nearly every round of golf I've played in the last 20 years. Purpose changes your perspective.

It's the same way with work; when we know why we do what we do, we can handle being "in the rough" from time to time. But if we're punching a clock only to get a paycheck, we'll burn out, resent our job, get very little satisfaction, and see very little success from the daily grind.

We can't make good decisions about God's purpose for our lives and our work without asking similar types of questions. For instance, have you struggled with your goal(s) in life? What do you most hope to accomplish in your time here on earth?

- Accumulate wealth?
- Become the best employee a company has ever seen?
- Contribute to the profitability of your company?
- Raise your children to become productive adults?
- Have a lot of friends?
- Just have fun?
- To love and honor God?

Have you established your goals? They're different for each one of us and multi-dimensional for most. Or maybe there's a better question. What constitutes success for you? When you get to the end of your life, how will you know if you've been successful?

Let me illustrate with a not-so-far-fetched example: A young business person quickly advances, moves into management, and ultimately becomes the president of a large organization, earning a salary of $300,000 a year. He marries, rears three children, sends them off to college, plans for the future, retires to Scottsdale, Arizona, and dies at the age of 79. Was he successful? If yes, why? If no, why not?

Perhaps by the world's standard he was very successful, but does the world's standard really matter? What promises does the world make to us? None! What about God's standard? What does He expect from us? This is where God's purpose for our life becomes important. There's one fundamental question we'd all be wise to ask ourselves: *Why am I here on earth?* The answer will have massive implications for our life and our work.

When asked, Jesus identified two commands as most important: *Love the Lord your God with all your heart and with all your soul and with all your mind and with all your strength. The second is this: Love your neighbor as yourself* (Mark 12: 30-31). That should give us some clues about His view of our purpose and what matters most to Him.

In Rick Warren's best-selling book, *The Purpose Driven Life,* he captures the essence of this view when he says that our ultimate purpose lies in glorifying God. He outlines five ways we can do that: worship God, love others, become like Christ, serve others with our gifts, and tell others about Christ.

~ *The* "purpose" question: What do you live for? ~

Regardless of whether you agree with Warren's list, each of us needs to understand the goal and purpose of our life so we can make choices in the right context. Otherwise, our career can easily become the central goal and purpose by default. Maybe that's why so many of us take our work too seriously and perhaps why work seems so empty to many. Worse yet, it might be the reason that, when we lose a job, we feel as though the most important thing in our life has been taken away. Is that what God intended for us to feel? It's doubtful.

We worry about career choices and jobs as if they are life- and eternity-defining issues. And yet, for the average person, many different careers could align with God's will for them. What God really cares about is that you use the gifts he has blessed you with and do it in a Christ-like manner that brings glory to Him. Work is not the end goal. It's a way for us to make a contribution, to earn a living, to develop our character and skills, and to serve and reach others. It's not the primary reason we're on this earth.

Until you take time to consider these broader life-purpose questions, you have no context to decide what's important in your life. Without understanding your purpose and priorities, the question "What career should I pursue?" is nearly impossible to answer because it becomes a random selection. On what do you base the considerations? What criteria do you use to evaluate options?

The best way to gain clarity of purpose in your work and in your life is to become intentional. These suggestions may help:

- Spend quiet time with God every day. It doesn't have to be more than 20-30 minutes at a time. Reading and studying scripture, journaling, praying, and reflecting are all proven methods for investing in your relationship with Christ, and the payoff is clarity about God's will and purpose for your life.
- Read *The Purpose Driven Life*.[22] It's a Bible-centered perspective on what it means to have purpose in your life, and it only takes 20-30 minutes per day for 40 days.
- Seek the counsel of those who are capable of mentoring you—those who have the experience and spiritual grounding to help guide your steps and provide counsel in the process. If you don't know

anyone who fits this description today, your church may be the most likely place to find them.

In this process, you'll want to spend the time needed to get comfortable (or maybe uncomfortable) with the answers to these fundamental questions:

- What is my purpose for living?
- Does it match God's perspective of my purpose?
- Within this context, what is the fundamental purpose of my work? Does it support my broader life purpose? (It should.)

Once you're comfortable with the answers, you can then explore the importance of understanding your calling by assessing your gifts and talents, your experiences, and your passions (Chapter 5). Then we'll identify the key priorities (Chapter 6) that become the final piece of the "context" puzzle to create a balanced work-life (Chapter 7).

God's view of work

In order to answer the second of the three questions above, we need to deal with another issue. How does God view our work? Is it a necessary evil? A punishment? The center of our existence?

Actually, it's none of the above. Work was ordained before Adam and Eve sinned; it was part of a perfect existence in the Garden of Eden (Genesis 2:15). But while the Bible discusses the importance and value of work, it doesn't suggest that it should be the central part of our life. Men particularly, myself included, seem more subject to putting our careers at the pinnacle of our existence.

So, how do we keep work in the right perspective—i.e., God's? Here are a few notable verses from scripture that should help:

- God sees work as important. *...If a man will not work, he shall not eat* (2 Thessalonians 3:10). God expects us to work and to do so with a good attitude. There's no easy way around the necessity of eating, making our house payment, and clothing ourselves and our families.

- At the same time, God doesn't see work as the "end all." In Exodus 20:3 He clearly commands, *You shall have no other gods before me.* And in Ecclesiastes 4:6, *Better one handful with tranquility than two handfuls with toil and chasing after the wind.* As soon as we begin to view work as the dominant part of our identity or our time, we risk violating God's will for our work. For many, the lure of money becomes the excuse for over-working – and the Bible is also clear to point out that we can't serve both God and money (Matthew 6:24). We can't allow our work to take the primary role in our life.

- God has a plan for us—an infinitely wise plan. *"For I know the plans I have for you,"* declares the Lord, *"plans to prosper you and not to harm you, plans to give you hope and a future"* (Jeremiah 29:11). God wants us to do work that's consistent with our gifts, talents, and experiences, and He expects us to have enough trust in His plan and provisions to know that if we're responsible and diligent, His grace and His care will protect us.

- God doesn't want or expect us to be miserable, even if the work we're doing doesn't perfectly suit our interests. Ecclesiastes 3:12-13 provides evidence, *I know that there is nothing better for men than to be happy and do good while they live. That everyone may eat and drink, and find satisfaction in all his toil- this is the gift of God*; and Colossians 3:23-24 says, *Whatever you do, work at it with all your heart, as*

*working for the Lord, not for man since you know
that you will receive an inheritance from the Lord
as a reward.* He has blessed us with talents and gifts
that are uniquely ours. He wants us to determine how
we can best use these talents to help meet our daily
physical needs and to use them in a way that glorifies
Him. How can you glorify God at work? Here's a few
important ways:

o   You can be joyful and thankful for the gifts you
    have, including the opportunity to work and earn
    money. The key to honoring God in your work
    may not rest in changing the work you do but
    changing your attitude about the work you do
    today.

o   You can view your work environment as your
    own personal ministry field. If we leave ministry
    and evangelism to our clergy, we miss a golden
    opportunity. In fact, if every Christian worker
    went to work every day with the goal of advancing
    Jesus' mission—treating people in a Christ-like
    way, sharing our knowledge and love of God's
    Word, or any other activity that would be consis-
    tent with the Great Commission—we'd have a
    radically different perspective on our work. What
    you normally do for yourself, you begin doing for
    God, including your work. Two excellent books
    can help in this regard: Regi Campbell's *About My
    Father's Business* provides great suggestions on
    how to fulfill the Great Commission at work in a
    simple, unobtrusive way; and *The 9 to 5 Window*
    by Os Hillman provides insightful perspectives
    on viewing our work through a Christ-centered
    lens.

o   Our work is also a great opportunity to serve
    those who work with us. Remember the second

greatest commandment Jesus gave us—love your neighbor as yourself? Too many people erect a thick wall between their work and the rest of life. Work is simply one element of life, and God expects our best in all we do. He wants whatever we do to honor Him, provide a clear example for others we work with, and ultimately allow us and others to grow closer to Him.

o Work allows us to develop our skills and to do whatever we do with excellence. Those who work hard and do great work tend to succeed. Those who don't, won't. God designed it that way.

Look again at Rick Warren's list of the five ways to bring glory to God for the gifts, blessings, life, and promise of eternal life He has given us:

- Worshiping God
- Loving other believers
- Becoming like Christ
- Serving others with our gifts
- Telling others about God

Where does work fit in this list? What?! It isn't listed? Surely it would make the top five, wouldn't it?

God doesn't care if we're successful in our work—*if* success is defined as maximizing profits, launching a new product, or getting all the shipments out the door on time and on budget. God's not impressed by our title or income. He provides us the work environment for *His* purposes: to accomplish His goals for our lives, to allow us to learn, to allow us to struggle, to allow us to be strengthened, and to glorify Him. Where we tend to see work as primary, God sees it as a means to an end—the "end," by His definition, is the degree to which we use every circumstance in our life to fulfill His purposes.

Work is really the opportunity for most of us to be "missional" Christians. We'll have significantly more opportunities to be on mission for Christ in our work lives than we could possibly hope to have on Sundays at church. Our workplace affords us a unique platform to represent God's character to the world around us. We can glorify Him there, develop our own character, learn greater new skills for greater usefulness in His kingdom, share our faith with others, demonstrate true servanthood, and display an eternal perspective. Work is a vital mission field!

~ God isn't impressed with our title... or income ~

Gary O'Malley is a friend who told me about one of the most profound questions he was once asked. "If you're a candy maker, is it alright to make candy just for the sake of making candy?" The world would say "yes." For the Christian, the answer is "no." We're called to do everything we do (work and play) to glorify God and fulfill His purpose for our lives. It's always made me cringe a bit when someone says, "I want to go into full time ministry work." The fact is we're all in full-time ministry work.

If you're highly frustrated with your work, your career prospects, or anything else related to work, and your frustration is having an overwhelming impact on your life, chances are that you've put your work ahead of God in your "statement of purpose"—if you have one at all. You're going to live for something in life. Will it be a career? A hobby? Fame and fortune? The key is to keep things in perspective and not allow the work you do to take on an exaggerated importance.

God's primary interest in our success has little to do with the business aspects of our work and everything to do with the extent to which He's honored in the process. We aren't ultimately responsible for outcomes anyway; that's His purview. What He wants is for us to commit and dedicate our work to Him—and to recognize that He's in control.

We tend to spend a lot of time and energy stressing about our work. Is that biblical? Not in the least. In fact, it's a violation of Jesus' instruction: *"Do not worry about your life, what you will eat or drink; or about your body, what you will wear. Is not life more important than food, and the body more important than clothes?"* (Matthew 6:25). God wants us to have faith in *Him* for all of our needs, not to obsess about how we'll get all the bills paid if we don't get all our work done or earn enough commissions. God knows our tendency is to worry and He'd rather we work faithfully and trust Him for the outcomes.

Converting Cruise Ships to Aircraft Carriers

The sacred-secular paradigm has grown deep roots in today's church, and breaking them constitutes a significant challenge. In order for the church and working people to join forces toward a common goal of serving others to God's glory and advancing His kingdom, the church must orient its function and focus on equipping its ministers in the workplace. Former business entrepreneur Doug Spada founded the non-profit venture *His Church at Work* (www. hischurchatwork.org) to support individuals and the church in this area. After a decade-long career serving on naval nuclear submarines, and many successful years in business, Doug experienced the Sunday-to-Monday disconnect and found himself completely frustrated and unable to connect with his calling. What he didn't know was that God would use this discontent with his church to birth a ministry that would bridge the gap between the church and others in the workforce just like him. Doug describes this new paradigm in churches as "converting cruise ships to aircraft carriers." He explains it this way:

> "Most churches have become like cruise ships. Those who attend are passengers. They're brought to the ship to be entertained and fed and then they return to their everyday lives. Instead of cruise ships, churches can aspire to become like aircraft carriers. The congregation isn't there for the program, they're on board to be taught, equipped, and refueled for a mission. The important work is done off the aircraft carrier, as fighter planes (individual believers) do battle wherever they're sent. As Nehemiah identified with the sin of the entire nation of Israel, we also must identify with the problem of the current cruise ship paradigm. We have been part of building and sustaining many of our cruise ship churches, not demanding a more biblical paradigm and metrics of success beyond attendance, budgets and buildings.

If you're intent on helping to bring your work's relevance to your church and your own faith walk, consider sharing this integrated life-vision with your church so that they can effectively equip believers for kingdom impact in the marketplace by contacting *His Church at Work*.

Attitude is everything

Life is full of choices: We can hold grudges...or we can forgive. We can be happy...or we can be unhappy. We can worry about everything...or we can relax and not worry. We can be envious of others...or we can be content with what we have. We're free to choose. Nobody forces us to feel anything; we decide on what we feel every moment of every day. If an employer treats you unfairly, you can feel hurt or you can let it roll off your back. You can stay, or you can leave. And you *should* leave if you find yourself in a work environment that's unbearable.

The point is that we all get to choose the attitude we have about our work—and about life, for that matter. Some people with the best jobs imaginable are very unhappy, while others, with jobs the rest of us would hate, enjoy their work. The difference has little to do with the job and everything to do with the attitude of the person in the job. Are you choosing happiness and contentment, or something else? I once heard a friend say, "If you don't like where you work, change your attitude first, not where you work"

Let's take a common challenge: working for a bad boss. Whether they're disrespectful, incompetent, or oppressive, bad bosses can really test our patience. They can also put a damper on more than just our work as we bring our frustration home and into our other relationships.

~ If you don't like where you work, change your attitude first, not where you work ~

What's the right approach to handle this almost inevitable situation? First, God gives us great advice on how to deal with those in authority over us - with respect - regardless of how unreasonable they are (1 Peter 2:18-23). Second, know that you have choices. We can be miserable and belligerent, or we can attempt to make the best of the situation and learn all we can about ourselves and how to deal effectively with those with whom we struggle. And finally, we can seek God's guidance as to whether we should look for a better alternative. God doesn't sentence you to a miserable job, company or boss, though He may intend for your current situation to be an opportunity for your personal development. As Romans 8:28 reminds us, *We know that in all things, God works for the good of those who love Him and are called according to His purpose.* The challenge lies in finding the purpose and the lessons in whatever work situation you're dealt.

If your frustration with work is having an overwhelming impact on your life, it may be that you've allowed work to control your attitude. If so, it's likely that either your attitude or your work situation needs to change.

The key to finding the best situation for you rests in your ability to do work consistent with your calling, your priorities, and God's purpose for your life. If those criteria are met—whether with a new attitude in your current employment or by transitioning to another job—your work will take on a new, more balanced place in your life, and your attitude will reflect it - to God's glory.

Interesting how we've come full circle back to our purpose in life, isn't it? When purpose is clear, everything else becomes a component of fulfilling that purpose. Our work is a significant part of our lives, and God equips us with everything we need to do His will. He doesn't waste our abilities. Our challenge is to identify and capitalize on those abilities. God may equip some of us to make a lot of money, and He expects us to be good stewards of the money He so graciously blesses us with. He may equip others to be great servants without the ability to create wealth in this lifetime. That's fine too. Unless we have a truly eternal perspective, issues of fairness in this life will drive us crazy. It's not about us. It's about how we can best serve God, and our work is simply one vehicle to do so.

Chapter 4 Reflection Questions

- What do you think God's perspective is regarding your work?
- Are you clear on your life's purpose? Does your perspective on your purpose align well with God's?
- What does God most expect you to accomplish with your work?
- What work-related steps can you take to better align your purpose with God's purpose for you?
- How would you describe your current attitude toward your work? How can it be improved? Even if you're planning to find different work, why might it be important to cultivate a different attitude in the meantime?

Chapter 5

Hear Your Calling (and Caller)

—∿∿—

Wouldn't you love to get up every morning with excitement because you have an opportunity to do exactly what you're equipped to do? Or to know that your work each day will accomplish something valuable and make a significant impact? Or to know you're heading down the right career path and are taking one more step in the direction God wants you to go? This may be a lofty set of goals, but too few people experience this.

Once you've truly wrestled with your purpose in life and have some semblance of clarity about it, you're better equipped to shift your attention to exploring the work that God has made *you* for (and *for* you). It isn't a matter of randomly finding a job to get excited about. The challenge is to discover the truth about your passions, your gifts, and your experience that, combined with God's will and plan for your life, allows you to pursue your calling.

Think of it like this: Just as there's a car for every person (I recall the commercial for AutoTrader.com with the guy who was elated that the puke-green '76 AMC Gremlin he found on-line was still for sale); and just as there's a house for every family (a family bought a house in our neighborhood that our friends and neighbors thought would never sell—and when I met the family who bought it, they excitedly proclaimed, "We were amazed this house was still available!"); in the same way, there's a job and a career (perhaps many) for every person. Case in point: my wife, Devonie, works part time in a small, quaint tea room. It's usually filled with ladies' chatter, tea, sandwiches, and laughter—a working environment I wouldn't last in for a week. She, on the other hand, thinks it's the greatest environment in the world. It's a matter of each person finding the right fit.

What am I called to do?

Most of us find it challenging to clearly (or even vaguely) answer the all-important question of our calling. That question is at the heart of finding the fit between what God has created you for and for you. Calling is about understanding yourself well enough—with all your greatest strengths and, yes, even your weaknesses—to know that you were designed for work that takes greatest advantage of your gifts. In essence, your calling is the manifestation of God's plan for your life and for your work.

As we struggle with the challenge and opportunity of our calling, it's worth pausing for a minute to consider the "caller." If we're called, someone must have called us. That someone is the Lord. We have a primary calling, and it's not all about us. Os Guinness says in his book, *The Call*,

> For the followers of Christ, calling neutralizes the fundamental poison of choice in modern life. "I have chosen you," Jesus said, "you have not chosen me." We are not our own; we have been bought with a price. We have no rights, only responsibilities. Following Christ is not our initiative, merely our response in obedience... Once we have been called, we literally "have no choice."[23]

Therefore, our primary calling is the call of Jesus on our lives. In all we do, whether work-related or not, we are called to serve Him. The choice is not ours and the promise is profound, *Therefore, my brothers, be all the more eager to make your calling and election sure. For if you do these things, you will never fall, and you will receive a rich welcome into the eternal kingdom of our Lord and Savior Jesus Christ* (2 Peter 1:10-11). This call of Jesus on our earthly lives has an eternal reward!

~ Do you understand your primary call from the ultimate "caller"? ~

As Guinness goes on to say, "You can retire from your job but not your calling. You can be unemployed but you are not uncalled."[24] Our calling actually transcends our work. This context is important to consider as we explore a few important principles:

- We're all called by God in some special way. That doesn't mean we're all going to be famous—or infamous, for that matter. It does mean that you can be encouraged that God has and will provide you with whatever is required to accomplish your calling.
- Our calling is usually consistent with our skills and interests. God built you the way He did for a purpose, and it's both logical and biblical to have confidence that He has equipped you according to His divine plan. It's also inconceivable to think that He wouldn't equip you at all. (Have you ever heard someone say "There's nothing I'm good at doing!"?) We all have a calling. It's just a matter of finding it.
- Your calling will likely fit several careers, not just one. Far too many workers feel they have to find the

one job they're suited to fill. We're all equipped with the gifts to do multiple jobs—so relax about finding *the* perfect job.

- Rest assured that your calling will not only serve you well, it will also fulfill God's purposes for your life and His Kingdom. In fact, all Christians are called to full time ministry in our work – to love and serve others.
- Finally, leave the "outcome" of your calling to God. Scott is a friend who felt called to work with a great ministry in New York. Before he accepted the position he asked the ministry leader, an innocent question, "Do you think I'm called to work with this ministry?" The leader responded, "I have no doubt that you've been called to this ministry, but neither you nor I know if you've been called to be successful." The point – sometimes we're called but "success" may be the journey itself, not the outcome or results.

My own career "calling" may highlight the challenges and opportunities involved. For the 30 years I have known my wife Devonie, I can remember periodically commenting to her that I felt I had a God-given talent and calling to teach. In fact, I've always enjoyed coaching, mentoring, and public speaking, and teaching contains dimensions of all three. But I always ruled out the possibility of school-based teaching because of my affinity for the business world and my priority of providing for my family and sustaining our standard of living.

While God was preparing me through specific work experiences, it wasn't until 18 years into my career that it became obvious that I could have my proverbial cake and eat it too. I could teach what I had been successful doing for most of my career - selling. I've been in sales in one form or fashion since graduating from college and I've always been a student of both the art and science of selling. So I finally left Andersen Consulting in 1998 to join a sales training and methodology organization in the Atlanta area called The Complex Sale. I love the work, it fits my talents and interests, and the clients I've worked with value my skills and our company's approach enough to pay me to do it! It's the epitome of what a calling is all about—in practical terms. And, it's my personal mission field – an environment where I can touch the lives of others for the glory of God. My prayer is that He will enable me to continue to do this type of work, in some form, until he invites me to our eternal home some day.

~ We're often "called" but not always called to be successful ~

There are other practical examples. Take Mike Pinzl as an example. He spent nearly 25 years with a Fortune 1000 company in operations and human resources. And while he looks back affectionately on his experiences and the relationships he developed there, he aspired to do something he could really enjoy. He resigned from his company—timed with a corporate layoff and at a point when he could give one of his kidneys to a brother badly in need of one—and started a small business in the north Atlanta suburbs called Uncle Shuck's Corn Maze. (It's literally a maze in a corn field that families can navigate during the Fall and Halloween season—complete with a pumpkin patch, pony rides, etc). He's figured out that he's an entrepreneur at heart and has grown this seasonal business to a point where he's making more money on a seasonal basis than he did annually with his previous employer. He is uniquely gifted for this business.

What about you? Do you have a clear view of what you're equipped and called to do? How can you take advantage of your unique skills? Where does your passion lie?

Seek God's guidance

It's easy to become too focused on our own vision for our future and the plans that we've developed for ourselves. The best way to get clarity on where God is calling us is to be prepared to "die to self"—to surrender our will to God. He made us. He's called us as the ultimate "caller". And He's fully capable of leading us—if we'll allow Him to do so.

God guides us through many means: scripture, prayer, reflection and quiet time, circumstances, and certainly through other people. Over time, if you're discerning and aware enough to see where God is leading you, you can usually gain insight into His purpose for your life and where He's calling you to serve. Your calling isn't a secret that He's reluctant to divulge. Discerning it, though, does require an investment of your time and energy. And our calling isn't limited to our job/career. If it is, and then we lose that job, we've lost our calling and perhaps lost touch with the ultimate caller.

~ Christians are called to full time ministry...in our work!~

Growing close to God and knowing His will don't simply come with a once-a-week visit to church. God desires an intimate relationship with us. Do you have daily prayer or Bible study time each day? Do you journal? If your desire is to learn God's will, it won't come at the warp speed most of us travel. I'm a testament to the notion that the more I slow down the pace of my life and my work, the more clearly I seem to grasp God's will for my life. Try it for yourself.

One more dimension of seeking God's guidance: don't underestimate the value and the power of surrounding yourself with godly people. Those around you are not only the most likely to influence you but also the most capable of giving you wise counsel as you struggle with direction.

Fostering these relationships is a great way to give yourself an opportunity to hear God's will, up close and personally.

The components of your calling

As you continue to seek God's guidance, you'll next make a personal assessment in three key components of your calling:

- Your gifts and talents
- Your passions
- Your experience and accomplishments

Ultimately, when you look at the intersection of these three dimensions, you'll begin to get a clearer view of your calling. You'll find a template on our web site (www.betterwaytomakealiving.com) to help you develop your personal inventory in these areas. Let's look at an overview of each.

Inventory your gifts and talents

Start by identifying the personal and professional gifts and attributes that have enabled you to succeed in your work and in your life. In essence, which of your skills have proven themselves?

- Your people skills and the ability to relate well with others?
- Your communications skills? Written? Verbal? Other languages?
- Your ability to work with numbers?
- Your ability to serve customers effectively?
- Your organizational skills?
- Your problem-solving abilities?
- Or one of hundreds of other attributes that people are uniquely blessed with?

Your challenge is to identify and embrace these attributes and then find the best way to apply them to your career. Most people possess a few key strengths that are most valued by the marketplace. I know what you're thinking: "But I've done 50 things well in my career!" I believe you; we all end up doing myriad tasks in our jobs. But the reality is that most of us are only exceptional at a few key skills. The secret is to make good use of these skills by establishing them as the key aspects of your current or future role—whether with the company you work for today or a new one.

You may benefit from a formal career assessment, now widely available through the Internet, to help you discern your key strengths. Career Direct (<u>www.careerdirectonline.org</u>) is a good example. It's developed by Crown Financial Ministries (<u>www.crown.org</u>), which works with churches throughout the world to help people learn to manage money in a biblically sound way and to be good stewards of God's gifts. Assessment tools like this are very helpful to gain an objective view of your skills, interests, and personality traits so you can identify job categories that fit you.

Inventory your passions and interests

Next, let's determine what really gets you excited, even if they're not the same as your gifts and talents. Here are a few self-assessment questions to get you started:

- What kind of work would you do for free if you had the luxury of not needing an income? (The goal, of course, would be to do it so well that others would gladly pay you for it!) There are no bad ideas at this stage of your personal inventory.
- At what times in your past (work, play, hobbies, etc.) were you the happiest and most fulfilled? What aspects of your previous jobs have been the most satisfying? What did you most enjoy about them?

- Are any dreams or aspirations planted in your heart that you've never really allowed to surface? Or do you feel that God has planted a dream within you that you've never really dealt with or discussed with others?
- Have you taken the time to clearly define one or more "perfect" roles based on what you've learned about yourself? For example, you might catch yourself saying, "If I could find a job like _____, I'd be totally content." Can you define your ideal work environment? Is it:
    - o As an individual performer or a manager?
    - o In a team environment or working independently (or from home)?
    - o With a large company or small?
    - o In a high-growth, fast-paced field or a "steady state" business?
    - o In a "high performance" culture or a more "people friendly" culture?
    - o With your manager down the hall or 2000 miles away?
- And finally, what truly draws on your emotions? Is there a cause that tugs at your heart? Perhaps a ministry or organization that you would love to spend your entire time helping? In other words, what brings tears to your eyes? Or, what fills you with true joy?

~ Your passions often reveal God's purpose... for you ~

God puts part of His own heart and will in those who love Him. These questions will go a long way toward helping you discover how He wants you to fulfill His purposes.

Outline your experience and accomplishments

Have you ever taken the time and energy to capture and document your most outstanding accomplishments? In your work life? In your personal life, including hobbies? In your spiritual life? If you haven't, it should be a very encouraging exercise. Most of us don't take enough opportunities to look back at what we've achieved. Try sharing your accomplishments with others who know you well (co-workers, your spouse, a close friend, etc.) and see what they would add or amend. Choose those who will give you honest feedback, not those who tell you what they think you want to hear. In essence, you need to have a clear view of what you've accomplished so you can leverage it going forward.

This is a critical dimension of this process because your ability to compete effectively for a new position, whether as an employee or independently, often depends on whether you can convince a potential employer that you have the requisite experience to be successful. I've witnessed many career explorers who try to pursue a career path outside of their previous experience, only to find that employers opt for a candidate that has more relevant or more direct experience in the trade or industry. That's not to say you can't transition to a completely different field; you aren't locked into a career simply because you've spent 10 years in that environment. But don't expect a lateral or upward move to a field in which you have no background. Acquiring skills takes time. Understand what your skill set and experience will do for you and what it won't.

Research career options

Once you've taken an inventory of your gifts, your passions, and your experiences, you can then evaluate your options in today's job market. Chapter Three highlighted some high-growth job categories, but there are additional ways to approach finding great career options.

First and foremost, be observant and inquisitive. The most curious people we meet are often those who find the best career opportunities. Literally thousands of careers could fit your skills, passions, and experience, but you can't pursue them if you don't know they exist. Lest you think it requires an extraordinary amount of time to discover your options, you can do a great deal of research from the comfort of your computer at home. It also doesn't take much time—plus, it's fun—to ask people you meet about their careers wherever you happen to meet them.

When you come across careers that seem to be a good fit for you, conduct informational interviews with a few people who have pursued those careers. Remember, this activity isn't limited to those who are in between jobs; it's a strategic habit every worker should embrace, even those who are content with their current job. Make it a habit to go to lunch with someone who has an interesting and/or unique career. Have a cup of coffee with another who can give you a head start down that particular road. Don't shortcut this part of the process. Get to know these people. Try to see—firsthand, if you can—where they do their work so you can get a sense of the environment. Find out all you can. People love to talk about themselves, and most want to give advice. You'll want to ask questions including:

- Why did you choose this career?
- What lessons have you learned since you started in this field?
- What do you like most about it? What do you dislike?
- What defines success in this job? What skills and resources are required to achieve success?
- Would you choose this career again?
- What advice would you give to someone like me who's considering a transition to this field?

Take advantage of the fact that people love to share their experiences! Your goal in this process is to understand all you can and get clarity not only about where you belong, but also the best path to get there. You'll find that the people who help you with the exploration process can also be incredibly helpful one day if and when you make the decision to make a change. Who knows? They may even help mentor you during your transition.

Useful resources

There are some valuable resources that can help you in your exploration process. Here are a few examples:

- The U.S. Department of Labor has a web site that provides the Occupational Outlook for thousands of careers. It has projections about new jobs, the skills and education required for them, and even the pros and cons of most careers (www.bls.gov/oco/home. htm).
- Local community college career centers are a great source of guidance and even contacts and job leads in the local market. They are free to use in most cities.
- Google (and other search engines on the Internet) may be among the best tools to help discover career opportunities – and there's no limit to the searches you can play with to uncover hidden "gems." Try a few searches for yourself: "unique careers," "high growth jobs," "jobs for stay at home moms," or even, "perfect jobs for introverts" (I recently saw 30,400 entries on Google for this search term).
- Crown Financial and its assessment tool, Career Direct (www.crown.org), can help you take a personal inventory of your interests, skills, and personality and then identify career options that fit well for you.

At this point, the challenge becomes finding the linkage (see figure below) between three key dimensions: your career calling (gifts and skills, passions and interests, and your experience); your priorities (which we'll cover in more depth in the next chapter); and today's job market opportunities. Ultimately though, we need to determine how they all fit within the broader context of God's "primary" calling for your life.

PURPOSE
(Our "Primary" Calling)

Calling
• Gifts/Talents
• Passion
• Experience

Priorities
• Spiritual
• Career
• Financial
• Family
• Personal development
• Community

Job Market Opportunities
• High growth jobs
• Unique jobs
• Geographic hot spots
• Specialty Skills
• Buy a franchise
• Other?

We're putting together the pieces of this puzzle to allow you to find the work and the life that God designed for you based on the unique way He made you. You'll be tempted to find all of the reasons that the ideas you come up with aren't good ideas. You may think, "I can't afford the cut in pay!" or, "I don't have the right training for that!"

Try to resist these objections at this point in the process. You're better off considering all options and eliminating some later than not considering them at all. And remember, where there's a will—especially if it's God's will—there's a way.

You're working through this process is to ensure that your work, whatever you may choose, fits well with what you're on this earth to accomplish—not simply related to work, but beyond - including your family, your faith, and, most importantly, your relationship with Jesus Christ. If you have clarity in your purpose, your calling, and the best job market opportunities, we're ready for the next chapter: a discussion on how your priorities fit into this equation. You may end up identifying a new career path or you may determine that your calling is better pursued within, or as an adjunct to your current career – perhaps even as a part-time avocation. Either way, you're taking steps in the right direction.

~ Purpose = your "primary" calling ~

I have walked this path personally and have come to learn that through a lot of time, prayer, and firsthand research and diligence, you will get a clear view of where you belong and what God is calling you to do for His glory. I'll confess that I get up most mornings and thank God for the blessing of His help and guidance in providing me with work that fits me well and gives me the sense of satisfaction that it does. There's a peace that comes with this clarity and I pray you'll find and enjoy it as well. Be patient and wait on God. He will reveal His will for your career and your life if you're diligent and thoughtful enough to seek His plans to get there. A great example of one couple's journey follows:

~ G.I. Joe Your Way to Work: Brian and Becky Savage ~

I met Brian when he and I worked together at Nynex (now Verizon) in Dallas, TX. He and his wife Becky were both born and raised in Texas. Brian, the adopted son of a medical doctor, was involved in athletics, acting, and choir, among other activities, before attending Baylor University. In his six years at Baylor, he earned degrees in business broadcasting, marketing and management information systems and earned his MBA.

Becky knew she wanted to be a teacher from an early age and she attended Stephen F. Austin University and earned her undergraduate degree in education. She taught at five schools over the course of ten years, predominantly with gifted children's programs. "I loved teaching," she recalls, "and I knew it would be a great career for raising children."

Armed with his business and technology background, Brian went to work in sales for a division of Nynex that sold personal computers to business customers. The business unit he was part of was ultimately sold to another company, at which time Brian was promoted to a director level position in the new company. While he was highly successful in sales, he struggled with the low satisfaction he derived from working for someone else. "I enjoyed the personal computer business and the customer relationships I developed, but I never felt I was in control of my own destiny." Brian felt vulnerable to potential layoffs at the troubled company and began to look for career alternatives.

That's where G.I. Joe enters the picture. Brian was a serious G.I. Joe fan as a child and became a collector of all things G.I. Joe as an adult, but he considered it to be only a hobby. Until 1992, that is. He became the victim of a corporate layoff in April of that year and after trying to find a new position during a challenging economic time he began to consider starting his own company. The dream he and Becky conceived was to develop a business focused on serving the needs of those with a passion for collecting toys. Although it was difficult to estimate the size of the market, they sensed an opportunity to provide valuable information related to trading sources, current prices, available models, and upcoming events like toy shows that G.I. Joe aficionados would care about.

"The economy was struggling at the time, the job market was weak, and we had not yet started having children, so we felt it was the ideal time to take some risk, particularly since Becky was still teaching" explains Brian. His entrepreneurial streak took hold, and he decided to start a monthly publication to serve the doll and toy collector market.

Their hunch was that they wouldn't make the same kind of income they had previously enjoyed, but they were willing to adjust their lifestyle and make some sacrifices.

Through an initial mailing to 20,000 people, Brian obtained 500 subscribers for their publication, *Master Collector*. That wasn't a huge number, but it was a reasonable start. By 1995, their third year in the new business, Becky had given birth to the first of their three children, and Brian approached the Hasbro Corporation, the makers of G.I. Joe, about making his newsletter a licensed part of their toy offering. Over the next year, Becky returned to her teaching position while Brian took care of their son at home while running their business. Soon business took off, and it became clear to them that they had made a great career choice. Hasbro soon asked Brian to organize and run the annual G.I. Joe convention, which draws several thousand attendees each year. He even began manufacturing licensed products for the

G.I. Joe Collectors' Club members. Even though this collector market was not very big, it was large enough to carve out a very specialized and profitable business. In 1997, Becky and Brian moved back to the Dallas-Fort Worth area and hired their first full-time employee. Unfortunately for them, the momentum of the Internet actually negatively affected the growth of their business. The mass channel of the Internet and auction sites like eBay severely impacted the original business they had developed so successfully. It was simply too easy for people to get G.I. Joe information and products elsewhere in the e-world.

In light of the challenges and shifting business conditions, the Savages changed their business model to include online action figure sales as well as publishing and conventions. Hasbro was so impressed with their work that in 2004, they asked Brian and Becky to start the Transformers Collectors' Club and to produce BotCon, a convention for Transformers fans and collectors. They both contribute to the success of the business—as do several other family members during peak toy seasons—and they're both able to work from home.

Brian reflects on the challenge of operating his own business: "We manage our costs carefully, and we have confidence that God will provide for our future. We've had some challenges, including living through Hurricane Fran in 1996 when we had to rely on our church's generosity of using their facilities to get our newspaper out, but we've always had faith that everything would be fine."

How does Brian compare this work environment with the world of corporate America, where he started? "The line between work and family is now blurred. My life is my work and my work is an integral part of my life. I'm always around my family; everyone gets involved in what needs to be done—we're all in it together," he explained with an obvious sense of satisfaction.

On the role faith has played in their journey over the past ten years, Brian says, "God has always been important in our lives, and this experience has strengthened our faith and our relationship with God. God's in control, we're not."

Making your own business work, particularly a new, never-before-tried business, takes hard work and commitment. But the fulfillment Brian and Becky have derived from the experience makes it worth the effort. Theirs is a great testimony to the power of pursuing one's passion. It may seem like a crazy idea at the start, but if Brian and Becky can make a living in the action figure business, perhaps you can find a creative way to make a living based on your God-given passion!

Lessons Learned

Brian summed it up well, "Determine who you are and what your God-given talents are, and then figure out how to make a living doing it, but make sure you can separate business decisions from ones driven by emotion. Many people can find a part-time way to try out their career dream before they dive into it full time. You just have to be brave enough to take risks and have faith. It sounds simple, but it sure has worked for us."

Chapter 5 Reflection Questions

- What has God called you to do in your work life? If you don't know yet, what specific steps can you take to find out?
- Is there any tension between your work calling and your broader life calling?
- Have you clearly defined your God-given gifts and talents so you can determine how you might use them in your current and/or future career?
- Who do you know who could help validate your gifts, talents, and passions and help you explore career options that leverage these skills?

Chapter 6

Priorities: Becoming Intentional in Work... and Life

—ᨆ—

Your purpose and calling are only part of the equation in making work and career decisions. By themselves, they ignore the important context represented by your personal priorities which tend to be impacted by things like your circumstances, your stage of life, and hopefully, by your faith.

A simple example is the person, let's say an accountant, who's frustrated with his career and has decided he's called to be an artist. The collision of priorities occurs when you realize that this person is married with three children and has monthly expenses that don't allow him to quit his job to become an artist next week. He can certainly make progress toward becoming an artist, but because of competing priorities (like having food on the table and a roof over his family's heads), he must approach his artistic calling and its timing prudently.

What about our faith as a priority? I once heard Sonny Newton, a senior executive at The Chick-Fil-A restaurant chain, say to a group of men at a Souly Business Retreat in North Georgia, "God is not a priority in my life." The room went dead silent for 15 seconds and no one dared look at each other. How could he say that in a room full of Christian men? He proceeded to say it again! He finally broke the deafening silence in the meeting with an incredibly powerful statement, "God is **the** priority in my life!" How's that for clarity about one man's priorities?

What about you? What are your priorities in life? Do you know? Are they clear to you and others? Do these priorities determine how you spend your time at work and beyond?

As a manager, I earned a reputation for asking my direct-reports, "What three over-riding priorities do you want to accomplish in the next 90 days in order to achieve your goals?" Far too often, they had no immediate answer because they hadn't really thought about the context of priorities. They could certainly tell me the myriad activities they were focused on accomplishing today or this week, but they couldn't easily answer my question about what's really important. And I'd continue to challenge them to answer this question every 90 days. If they couldn't, it was a strong hint that they were activity-oriented, not priority-oriented.

What's the difference between the activities you're expected to do and the priorities you actually have? One (activities) is a "to-do" list that may or may not fit the overall purpose of your role, while the other (priorities) is the big-picture focus that should be guiding the "to-do" list in the first place. It's not unusual for a person's time and energy to be taken up with activities that were relevant a month or even a year ago but that no longer fit the organization's (or your) primary objectives. More work, less focus.

> **~ What priority are you intent on accomplishing in the next 90 days? Do you have one, or more? ~**

One way to determine if your time is in alignment with your priorities is to take an inventory of your activities from the previous month. As you look back at last month on your calendar (work and personal), was it filled with random activities that were largely in reaction to the issue *du jour*, or was it focused on achieving your top priorities? As often as not, your busyness is not aligned with your priorities, and the reason is simple: we all get caught in the activity trap. The bad news is that this also applies to our life outside of work, if we let it.

Priorities — the fence posts of life choices

Let's apply the concept to our careers: many people who have been in a job with one company for a long time (some even 30-plus years) continue to do the same work they've done, regardless of how unfulfilling it has been, often because they haven't taken the time to ask, "What's really important to me?"

We get caught in what Stephen Covey refers to in his book, *The Seven Habits of Highly Effective People,* as the "urgent, not important" quadrant of activity. He argues that we spend relatively little time in the "not urgent, important" quadrant, which includes things like planning our career, developing our skills, focusing on the important relationships in our lives, and other activities that are critical for ensuring that we're investing our time and energy in what is really important in our lives.

	Urgent	Not Urgent
Important	**I** ➢Crises ➢Firefighting ➢Deadline Driven Projects	**II** ➢Relationship Building ➢Personal Development ➢Spiritual Development ➢Career Planning
Not Important	**III** ➢Interruptions ➢Some Mail ➢Some Meetings	**IV** ➢Some Mail ➢Time-wasters ➢Pleasant Activities

Covey, Stephen R., The 7 Habits of Highly Effective People, New York: Simon & Schuster, 1989

The most comfortable thing for many of us to do is the same thing we've done in the past, especially if we've been doing it for a long time. Change is hard, especially when it comes to our careers.

Try this- take a minute to rank these ten items in order of importance in your life:

- Children
- Church
- Civic duty
- Self
- Health
- Spouse/marriage
- Work
- Friends
- God
- Finances

How did you do? Was it hard or easy? The tougher questions may be: How well does your time align with these priorities? And, how well does your career align with these priorities? For example, if family is one of your top priorities, does your current career allow you to spend enough time with them? If God is your number one priority, how much time do you invest in developing your knowledge of and relationship with Him? I think you get the point.

When I challenged myself to ask these questions, I wasn't proud of the answer. Specifically, my number one priority is serving and glorifying God, but I was spending no less than 60 hours of most weeks trying to maximize profits for my employer and almost no time developing my relationship with Jesus Christ. I had compartmentalized God into a convenient Sunday morning box. As I focused more on understanding and embracing my priorities, it became increasingly impossible for me to believe that God wanted me to use my gifts and talents in such a lopsided fashion. That's why I changed career tracks—twice. It's also why it's so important to regularly examine our priorities.

Ask yourself a few more questions on your broader life goals and priorities:

- What two or three major goals do I have for my life? (The answer may or may not have anything to do with your current work)
    - o Career goals?
    - o Personal goals?
    - o Family goals?
    - o Financial goals?
- Fill in your answer(s) for "X" in the following statement: "I will be disappointed if I don't accomplish X in the next five years."
- As mentioned in chapter 4, perhaps the most important "priority" question for all of us to answer: What's my purpose (and God's purpose for me) in life? Does the answer align with your answers above?

Without these answers, you have no roadmap. Any old road will do, regardless of where you intend to end up. In the same way, without knowing what you want to accomplish and what your priorities are, any old job will do. In essence, you have no fence posts to keep you traveling in the right direction instead of a random course.

On the other hand, armed with thoughtful answers to these questions and the context they provide, you're far better able to identify the boundaries that will help determine your best career and life choices. When our purpose, priorities, and the work that takes up most of our time and energy don't align, frustration (or worse yet, misery) is the result. How else can you discern the career that aligns with your priorities?

~ "I will be disappointed if I don't accomplish X in the next five years." Do you have an answer? ~

Consider a couple of simple examples to illustrate this alignment. First, there's "Mary," a 30-year-old woman who's married and has two children under the age of 5. If Mary consciously decides that her purpose and priority in life are centered around being a loving wife and nurturing mother of her two young children, with the goal of raising these children to be productive adults who know and love Jesus as their Savior, she will struggle with work that forces her to work long hours and put her children in day care from 8 a.m. to 5:30 p.m. each weekday. She may be fulfilled in her work, but she'll have a large hole in her heart because she's missing what she determined to be a major priority for this stage of her life. She'll be discontent at a minimum.

For another example, consider "Mike." He's a 40-year-old businessman with a gift and passion for music. In fact, one of his dominant priorities is to use his music skills to minister to others, particularly in Sunday church services. The challenge he faces is that his job requires him to work two or three weekends a month, which limits his ability to fulfill this priority. He makes a good living in his job but feels conflicted about his competing priorities. Until Mike aligns his priorities with his choices, he'll struggle.

Without considering the broader priority and purpose questions, we'll often feel unrest. To reconcile the inner turmoil requires alignment between your choices and these all-important priorities. These additional questions can help define your priorities:

- If rearing our children to be healthy, productive, and faithful adults is a high priority, how important is it to have one parent at home when they get home from school?
- If family time is a high priority, how much are you willing to travel?
- Is it important to reduce your dependence on a single company for your livelihood? What alternatives could you pursue to reduce this dependence?
- Which is more important to you: high income or high personal satisfaction in your work? Do you have either today?
- How many hours per week are you willing to work? Are you exceeding that today? If so, what is compromised as a result?
- How important is it to you to make a contribution to improve the world – in ministry or otherwise? Does your current work allow you to do that? Or does it provide you enough time outside of work to do so?

The answers to these and other relevant questions should inform your decisions on the best ways for you to make a living, and more importantly, a life. Not understanding your priorities seems to me like traveling cross country without a map. You'll get somewhere, but not where you're intending to go.

Let's look at the Priorities Roadmap™, a simple model to help you identify your priorities in relationship to each other—because they're all interrelated at some level and can't be considered independently.

Priorities Roadmap ™

Priority Dimensions	Self assessment	Key Goals	Action Items	Time Commitment/ Implications
Career				
Financial				
Marriage/ Family				
Personal Development				
Community Relationships				
Spiritual				

To complete the Priorities Roadmap, start by identifying and considering your most important categories. You may choose to add or replace a few categories to those listed above, although be careful not to create too many priorities (which can defeat the purpose of the exercise).

The first column of the matrix starts with a self-assessment. How important is each category—is this a critical priority or a low priority? What are your personal strengths and weaknesses related to each priority? How satisfied are you with your current position and your progress in each category? Is it a focus area of your life today? Should it be? It's important to be as objective and honest as you can because it's easy to make ourselves believe all is well in a category when, in fact, there may be some underlying challenges and opportunities to deal with.

A recent, notable example was a gentleman I met who believed all was well with his marriage. Then he and his wife went through a marriage workshop where both were asked to rate the strength of their marriage on a scale of 1-10 (10 being "best"). He rated their marriage a "9," she rated it a "2." This man either had his head in the sand or wasn't honest with himself (or his wife). An honest assessment will give you a much more accurate picture to work with to identify your priorities – and subsequent goals.

The second column is somewhat dependent on the self-assessment. For those categories that are most important (and that you are most focused on improving), identify the key goals you can establish to make progress. Be as specific as you can, and make it as measurable as possible (see examples outlined below for each category).

The third step is to define the specific action items that will allow you to achieve your goals in a reasonable time frame. This represents the "who," "what," and "when" of the process.

~ All priorities are not created equal: major in the majors! ~

Finally, assess the time required to achieve your goals and action items. Will it be a major time commitment that will have a significant impact on other priorities? If so, take this into account as you decide what can reasonably be accomplished. You can't afford to over-commit—you'll be doomed to failure in one or more categories.

You'll find a blank template of this Priorities Roadmap™ on our website (www.betterwaytomakealiving.com) to work through this exercise. It won't be an easy exercise when you begin but when you use this tool regularly, it becomes your permission slip (or the fence posts) that help you decide what choices to make in work and in life. You'll become far more intentional, rather than reactive to the barrage of life's daily activities.

Your priority categories and the goals associated with them will change over time. A recent college graduate will be driven by far different priorities and goals than a young couple with two young children. In the same way, a middle-aged family will be driven by a different set of work and life issues than an empty-nest couple planning for retirement.

Let's dig deeper into each of these categories to help you consider both the importance and possible implications before you develop your roadmap.

Career

By itself, making a career assessment and defining your career goals seems straightforward. But in the context of the rest of your life's priorities, compromises become important. In fact, when you compromise thoughtfully and proactively, you have a far higher probability of being satisfied in your choices and your circumstances rather than feeling victimized like so many do. Here are some practical questions and examples to consider as you complete this portion of your roadmap:

- Self-assessment questions/considerations:
    - o How important is my career in the scheme of my life? Why?
    - o Am I doing work that I feel gifted to do?
    - o Do I currently enjoy my work and career? Why or why not?
    - o Does my current career support my other priorities or compromise them?
        - Steal too much time from other areas?
        - Support our financial needs?
        - Support or compromise my ethics/beliefs?
    - o Could I do this work for the rest of my working life? Or do I aspire to something new or different?
    - o Is my current work a stepping stone to where I ultimately aspire to be?

Based on your answers to these questions, you'll begin to clarify the degree to which your current work/career aligns with your career priorities. And based on your answers you can begin to define some key goals that allow you to make progress in this area. If you are perfectly satisfied with all aspects of your current position and your career-related trajectory, this portion of the roadmap will reflect that and will help you to either "stay the course" or determine what adjustments should be made. Consider some examples of career goals:

- Key Goals:
    - o Earn a certification or license by next year to increase my responsibility or income.
    - o Get a promotion within two years

o Find a better company to work for (in the same line of work) that's a better cultural fit and shortens my commute.
o Embrace my work as a mission field to share my faith.
o Begin to do some independent contracting after hours to reduce my dependence on my current employer.
o Start my own business by January.

Once you establish one or two key goals for this category, you can then define the specific action items to achieve them. A simple example of an action item related to the first goal above (earn a certification) may be:

- Action Item:
    o Enroll in an evening certification class that starts in June (6 month class) at Anytown Community College.

Finally, it's important to then determine the implications of your chosen priorities and action items on your other, often competing priorities. This is where the compromising begins. The key here is honestly and objectively choosing the right priorities and ensuring that you allocate the time and energy they deserve, often at the expense of other priorities.

- Time commitment and implications - here are some examples in this "career" category:
    o If I enroll in a certification class, I'll have less time for my family during these next six months.
    o I'll also have less time for exercise and sleep.

o I'll have to stop attending Tuesday evening Bible study for six months.

I think you get the idea—nothing happens in a vacuum. When you focus on one area, it's bound to impact others, and that's okay. The challenge for you is to become proactive and intentional in making these choices, not reactive and unintentional. I remember when Devonie and I decided that I should pursue my MBA back in 1983 when I was with IBM. Our first child, Kelly, was an infant, and we knew the degree would be a minimum two-year commitment, mostly involving evening classes and studies. We decided it was worth the tradeoff, and I embarked on the program. Because of competing family priorities (two more children) and a one-year job transfer in the middle of the program, I ended up taking four years to complete the MBA. I'm grateful to have had the learning experience, and it has proven useful in my career since then.

Financial

This category may have the most profound impact on other priority categories because money often dictates (sometimes excessively) our choices and our flexibility. For example, the more you and your family are financially obligated, the fewer choices you tend to have. If you're saddled with significant debt payments and your income is less than your monthly expenses, you don't have the ability to quit your job and follow a calling that pays less. Faced with this circumstance, the imperative may be to work as hard as possible in the short term and get your costs and debt in line with your income. It becomes the first order of business and enables your career flexibility down the road. Let's look at other examples:

~ Priorities are the "permission slips" for our chosen activities ~

- Self Assessment:
    - o Are my current costs of living excessive or reasonable? (It may be worth asking a trusted advisor to help answer this question objectively)
    - o How much debt do I have, and does it impact my life and career choices?
    - o Do I earn enough currently to support my family?
    - o Do my income requirements make it hard or easy to change jobs? Do I feel trapped where I am?
    - o Have I set financial goals for:
        - Savings?
        - Tithing?
        - College fund?
    - o Am I meeting these financial goals?
    - o Do I track my current expenditures and know how and where I spend?
    - o Am I financially preparing for: post-retirement? A future health crisis within the family? Disability? Or a death to the working spouse(s) in our family?

Your financial goals should then be established based on this assessment and will be targeted to address your view of the most important of these priorities. Here are some sample goals (and sample action items/commitments) you may define:

- Key Goals (and sample action items):
  - o Increase earnings in the short term. (Work overtime to close our income/expense gap until I find a better paying job.)
  - o Land a new job by next year. (Begin my job search this month.)
  - o Retire all of our credit card debt within 18 months. (Enroll in Crown Financial Ministry's, "Managing Your Money" workshop this month.)
  - o Reduce our expenses by 10 percent. (Cancel cable TV, sell a car and buy an older one with no payments.)
- Time commitment and implications of these goals:
  - o If I work extra hours to retire debt, it will impact family time, Sunday church may be compromised, etc.
  - o If I reduce expenses, I may have less exciting vacations.
  - o If my short-term focus is on retiring debt, I'll have less flexibility to change careers during the next two years.
  - o On the positive side of the equation, lowering my overall expense will likely give me more career flexibility and more peace (and less stress).

Marriage/family

Most people insist that this category is among their most important priorities yet it often gets the proverbial short end of the stick when we allocate calendar time. If you're like me, you know that when there are struggles and challenges within your marriage and/or family, it usually has a profound impact on your effectiveness and productivity in work and many other aspects of life.

Too often we tend to focus primarily on our children as a priority and take our marriages for granted. This is backwards both practically and biblically. God is clear that the most important earthly relationship we have is with our spouse. He goes so far as to say that through marriage, the two individuals shall become one—physically and spiritually (Matthew 19:6). The best gift we can give our children is the gift of a great marriage. Is your marriage the priority it deserves to be? If it is, it will require an investment of time on your part and many other priorities—your children, your career, your finances, and your relationship with Christ—will be well served if you get this one right.

Let's look at the priority dimensions of marriage and family:

- Self-assessment:
    - o How do I assess our marriage? How does my spouse? (Have you asked?)
    - o How well do we model a God-centered marriage for our children? What can we do to improve?
    - o Do our kids face any challenges that I can't address sufficiently because of work-related demands on my time?
    - o How well do my spouse and I balance and compromise our careers for the benefit of the family?
    - o How much quality time is our family able to spend together? Could we increase it?
    - o Does our extended family have unique demands (aging parents, etc.) that require more time?
- Key Goals (and sample action items):

- o Revitalize romance and intimacy in our marriage. (Attend a marriage retreat in the fall)
- o Improve my children's education/school situation. (Evaluate home schooling and private school options within 90 days)
- o Find a way to have Mom stay at home with the kids for the next five years. (Downsize our house to lower our monthly expenses, if necessary)
- o Help our 17-year-old son overcome his drinking addiction. (Be home from work by 4:00 every day to begin to re-build my relationship with him.)
- o Care for our aging parents indefinitely. (Finish a basement to accommodate them in our house.)
- Consider once again the time commitment and the impact on other priorities:
  - o My career may take a backseat to several priorities above, at least in the short term.
  - o I (or my spouse) may need to work half-time or, at the other extreme, take on a second job to help pay the bills.
  - o I may have to change jobs to accommodate the demands of the family.
  - o The family savings plan may be put on hold during these demanding times.

These can be challenging issues with no easy answers. You'll have competing priorities in life and you're likely seeing a consistent message: you have to consider a better way to make a living...and a life in the context of your broader set of life's priorities.

Personal development

This is one priority that is in the "important, not urgent" category mentioned earlier in this chapter and, therefore, often gets trumped by more urgent priorities. When we don't invest in ourselves, many other priorities (including our effectiveness in our career) are compromised.

- Self Assessment:
    - o Am I physically fit? Do I have plenty of energy or am I often tired?
    - o Am I intellectually challenged at work—and otherwise? Am I learning new skills? Gaining knowledge?
    - o Do I have hobbies and outside interests that I wish I had more time for?
    - o Do I get enough rest and relaxation (margin!)?
- Key Goals (and example action items):
    - o Lose 30 pounds this year. (Start exercising 30 minutes/day, four times per week.)
    - o Read three books for pleasure and/or personal development this year. (Read the first one by end of the next month.)
    - o Earn a master's degree in Spanish. (Enroll in an Internet-based program this year.)
    - o Play golf once a month. (Invite my son each time.)
- Time commitment and impact on other priorities:
    - o These priorities may take time away from work. (Although they may actually increase productivity through better balance and/or energy.)
    - o I may have to change jobs to reduce my stress and hypertension.

o Can I choose activities that other family members can also enjoy?

Community and other relationships

This category includes civic organizations, church affiliation and relationships, and your broader network of industry and personal relationships that are important to nurture over time. Much of our professional, practical, spiritual and emotional support comes from relationships beyond just our family relationships. You'll also find that this set of priorities may take on greater relative importance at different life stages. For example, single people and married couples without children or those with grown children may have more time (and energy) for this priority than a family with three young children at home. Let's consider a few of these dimensions:

- Self-assessment:
    o Am I involved in efforts or causes that I'm passionate about? If not, why not?
    o Am I involved in church activities and/or a small group at church?
    o Do I feel that I'm contributing in any way to people or charitable causes outside of my family and work?
    o How strong is my network of contacts—both personally and professionally? Should it be better?
- Key Goals (and sample action items):
    o Get more involved in my church. (Join the women's club this month.)
    o Start a small group Bible study. (Get counsel from church pastor on best approaches and begin inviting people within 60 days.)

o   Get involved in a charity as a volunteer. (Call the United Way this month to find opportunities.)
- Time commitment and impact on other priorities:
    o   As I get increasingly involved in these types of activities, something else will likely be compromised—family, work, etc.
    o   Some of these activities may cost money and will impact my financial priorities.
    o   Many of these activities will actually benefit my career in terms of networking with contacts, getting advice and counsel, etc.

I witnessed a simple example of the interrelationships between these types of priorities and activities a few years ago when Devonie and I decided to get involved in mentoring engaged-to-be-married couples at our church as part of a formal ministry called "2-to1." We were concerned about the amount of time it might take and whether we were well-equipped for the ministry. Although it has compromised somewhat our time with our family and friends, we've found that the entire process of preparing ourselves and conducting the mentoring has been a tremendous blessing to our marriage—maybe even more so than to those we mentored! It's one of those mysterious and wonderful ways God works!

Spiritual

Last and perhaps most importantly, is the spiritual dimension of our priorities. For the Christian, this category should be the centerpiece of the priority equation. If we live *in* the world but not *of* the world, could anything be more important than our relationship with God? And yet, how often is our relationship with God the foremost consideration in our life and career decisions? Honestly, how much of our time is taken up by this priority? Probably not as much time as God longs for.

The imperative is to keep an eternal perspective about our work, recognizing that life and work are temporary (albeit a relatively long "temporary" if we live to 80 or 90). Matthew 6:33 says it well, *But seek first His kingdom and His righteousness, and all these things* (i.e. your other priorities) *will be given to you as well.* We are passing through this world in order to be with our Father in heaven for eternity. Why wouldn't we focus an enormous amount of our time and energy—in both our work and in our play—in preparing to be with Him?

~ For the Christian, the spiritual realm is *the* priority– is it for you? ~

I'm still a work-in-process but the more I grow in my knowledge and relationship with Jesus and the more I relinquish control of my life and circumstances, the more I experience the peace that God has promised, and the more both work and life are manageable and fulfilling.

Consider these questions:

- Self-assessment:
    - o Do I feel restless and unsettled in life? Or am I truly at peace?
    - o Am I certain about my future after I die? Or do I still have doubts?
    - o Do I feel closer to God this year than I did last year? Why or why not?
    - o How much time do I spend quietly with God each day? Is it enough?
    - o How well do I understand scripture and how it can apply to everyday life?

- o How clear do I feel about God's purpose for my life? Does this purpose pervade all of my work and activities?
- Key Goals (and sample action items):
  - o Spend quiet time with God every day. (Wake up 30 minutes earlier to read the Bible and journal.)
  - o Have family devotional time each evening. (Use *My Utmost for His Highest* to guide us.)[25]
  - o Become a student of God's Word. (Join a Bible study this quarter.)
  - o Join a church. (Attend services weekly.)
  - o Learn to pray *continuously*. (Get book recommendations from friends.)
- Time commitment and impact on other priorities:
  - o If I go to church, it's likely to impact my Sunday recreation.
  - o As my faith grows, I'll likely be more inclined to have a biblical perspective on life's priorities—and the decisions I make about my career will be influenced accordingly.
  - o I'm likely to feel less need to control my own circumstances and more likely to relinquish control to the only one capable of having it—God!

Guiding principles

When you consider priorities, it's always helpful to think about their relative importance. I know of few people who have only one or two dominant priorities. Most of us actually have several. How do you best reconcile these competing forces and still keep your life peaceful and balanced? A few guiding principles may help:

- *Major in the majors*. We all have a tendency to try to accommodate all of our commitments, activities, and priorities – all of which leads to the out-of-control symptoms we experience daily. The antidote: Limit your assessment of priorities and the corresponding goals and action items to the few, most important priorities (more like six than 16). By doing so, you'll have a better chance of allocating time to what really matters (the majors), not what doesn't (the minors). You'll also have to learn to just say "no" to whatever doesn't fit into the majors.
- *Don't sacrifice the eternal for the temporal*. If you face a choice between spending your energy and resources on something that lasts forever (eternal) and something that doesn't (temporal), it only makes sense to invest for the long term. (And think of the compound interest on an investment with eternal returns!) That's essentially what God promises for those who bear fruit in His kingdom. An example of the tradeoff: an afternoon invested with your teenage daughter (eternal investment) versus an afternoon spent with your golf buddies (temporal).
- *Align your priorities with your calendar - proactively*. If you review last month's calendar and determine that you spent your time on activities that don't align with your key priorities, you're likely in the activity trap mentioned early in this chapter. Changing your habits isn't easy, but it will never happen if you don't first define your priorities and establish the fence posts that allow you to be intentional in the process. In essence, this process gives you permission to say "no" to less important activities.
- *Align with your other key "stakeholders."* We all have plenty of other stakeholders and influencers in our lives—both in and out of work. When you

evaluate your priority roadmap, it's imperative to openly discuss and even strategize these choices and priorities with a few of the most important of these stakeholders. The logical few likely include your spouse, your mentors and/or trusted advisors, your boss (at least with elements of this roadmap), and perhaps even your children. The more the people that matter most to you understand and feel ownership for these choices, the more supportive they will be day-to-day.

- *Re-assess your priorities every 90 days.* Work and life are ever changing. Circumstances change, your life stage evolves, and your priorities should be rearranged as well—or at least be re-validated. Take the opportunity every 90 days or so to look again at your priorities to determine what adjustments, if any, are required to align your priorities with your time and energy.
- *Measure your success:* Progress will improve your work/life balance in tangible ways. We'll explore how to measure your progress more in-depth in the next chapter.

You'll read below the very personal story of the Delaplane's whose experience highlights how priorities can change everything in a family's life. Then, let's take this discussion on priorities and the guiding principles outlined above and explore in the next chapter the best, most time-proven approaches to creating the ever-elusive work-life balance that can enable you to obtain God's promised sense of peace in work and in life.

~ Tragedy rearranges priorities: Gary and Elvira Delaplane ~

In the 1970s and early '80s, corporate America was still fairly paternalistic, promising a career and long-term employment, a reasonable pension at the end of 30 or so years, and an invitation to the annual picnic, weather permitting.

Elvira, a native of New York City, left the big city to attend college in Tennessee and later worked as a flight attendant for TWA for 13 years. Gary, raised in rural Indiana, had earned a degree in chemical engineering and joined the DuPont Company in 1973. The two met and married in Kansas City where their older son Aaron was born. A few months after Aaron's birth, the couple moved to Buffalo, NY where two years later, Nathan was born.

Gary's career included stints in manufacturing, technology, sales, and research and development. In his words, "It was a good company that was well-respected, but, with the exception of two or three positions over a 28-year career, it was not particularly fulfilling."

Gary was the classic "company man," moving from position to position, learning new skills, and helping wherever the need existed. Moving his family with regularity, Gary's focus for most of his time with DuPont was on making his contribution to the company. Everything else took a back seat: "Looking back, I can now see that I was using my career as a feeble attempt to prove my personal value."

Then, through a series of what he refers to as "defining moments," Gary and Elvira's lives began to change—initially for the worse. In 1996, they were asked to relocate to Atlanta, their third move in four years. The house the Delaplane's bought in a suburb of Atlanta

141

turned out to be defective. "Over the next three years, we spent $52,000 in legal fees and another $15-18,000 in repairs, neither of which we could afford," explained Gary. The house became a source of additional stress in the Delaplane's marriage. "The pressure of work, ever-increasing expenses, the hassles with the house, and the challenge of raising teenagers made for a very stressful environment, and we weren't handling it well."

Their family was struggling. There was little closeness in their marriage. Nathan and Aaron were growing up, living separate lives, and not communicating with their parents. To escape the chaotic environment, Aaron left home to work at the Grand Canyon following high school; Nathan was still in high school at the time.

Then, in late 1997, came the revelation that changed their lives. Gary explained, "God spoke to my heart – 'enough is enough.' In that moment I realized that I had spent 30 years of my adult life trying to prove that I wasn't poor white trash from Indiana. I asked God to 'take over' my life, our marriage and our finances." With that submission, the healing process began. The couple joined a small group at church that worked through a curriculum on marriage intimacy. The lines of communication began to open. They began to pray together, they became faithful in tithing to the church, and, by 1999, there had been so many positive changes in their lives that they almost felt normal again. Then came the ultimate defining moment.

On May 4, 2000, Nathan, then 19, took his own life. "He was a special child in so many ways, but we found out later through his writings that he had kept so many of his feelings and frustrations bottled up inside of him," Elvira reflected. "It really made us reevaluate our lives, our priorities, everything."

Nathan's suicide was impactful in many ways. His writings have touched the lives of nearly 30 young people his parents know of, and likely many more. "Nathan helped us put a whole different perspective on our lives," Gary recalls. "My job, in particular, took on a different perspective - people at work who had issues began sharing with me like they never had before." Gary had long wanted to be a mentor or a coach to others, and his son's tragedy provided a platform for that. He and Elvira began ministering to others, initially to a colleague whose son had committed suicide. "God was beginning to make it clearer where I belonged," Gary says.

While Gary had expected to stay with DuPont until he reached full retirement age, that plan changed. In January 2001, he and Elvira began to adjust their lives to fit their priorities. They both felt called to work with couples whose marriages and families were struggling. They moved out of their large house, with its equally large mortgage, started to reduce other living expenses, and decided in July 2001 to take advantage of an early retirement package that DuPont offered. They didn't have a large monthly pension, but Gary and Elvira believed God would bless their willingness to re-prioritize their lives.

In addition to hosting marriage workshops with Gary in the evenings, Elvira began working as a substitute teacher in elementary schools. Gary completed a master's degree and is now licensed as a Christian counselor. They now work together and have founded a marriage counseling ministry called Mourning Dove Ministries (www. mourning-dove.org). They feel called to use their positive experiences and their trials to serve others and help them avoid the same mistakes.

They're a great testament to following your passions and using whatever platform God provides. This couple experienced marital strife, the loss of a child, and plenty of other trials. They now have a tremendous platform of credibility to talk with other married couples about what God has taught them.

"Life is good," says Gary. "We have found our purpose, and we have an opportunity to see change in people every day. No one is controlling our schedule. We love the flexibility in our lives and our ability to help others." Elvira adds: "We don't spend as much money as we used to, but we don't miss it because we traded it for more freedom of will and time."

Lessons Learned

Gary: "Nothing's more important than God, marriage, and family, in that order. Everyone should ask themselves why they are pursuing what they are. If it's not in line with their priorities, change."

Elvira: "You only have today; we're not promised tomorrow. Make the best of today. Life is all about relationships; everything else is a distraction. If we don't focus on our relationships, we'll have regrets."

Chapter 6: Reflection Questions

- Have you defined your top priorities in life?
- Does your calendar (time allocation) match these priorities? How closely do your stated priorities (what you say is most important) line up with your actual priorities (what you spend time and energy on)?
- Where does your career priority fit into your overall list of life's priorities?
- If your work-life feels out of balance, what steps can you take to create better balance?

Chapter 7

Center Yourself for Work/Life Balance

—ᶰᵐ—

There are six days when you may work, but the seventh day is a Sabbath of rest, a day of sacred assembly. You are not to do any work; wherever you live, it is a Sabbath to the Lord. —Leviticus 23:3

How's your work/life balance? You be the judge:

- How often do you bring work home from the office? During the week? On the weekends?
- For those who work from home, how often do you sneak into your home office to check your e-mails "one last time" for the evening? Or in the middle of the night when everyone else is sleeping?
- How many hours do you *really* work in an average week? Are you counting them all?
- Are you guilty of checking your voice and email messages in the bathroom (A recent Nokia survey showed that 53% of us do)?
- How well do you sleep on Sunday evenings compared to other nights of the week? Pretty restless? And

when do you start mentally gearing up for the coming week? Sunday evening? Sunday at lunch? Saturday night?

- When's the last time you went on vacation without spending a few hours on e-mail, conference calls, or reviewing documents?
- Do you ever feel unable to keep up with work *and* all of the activities you and your family are committed to — school activities, soccer and softball practice for the kids, or an upcoming church retreat?

Are you guilty as charged? I'll confess and I know I'm not alone. We are, as a society, running harder than ever. We run hard to achieve our individual objectives. We run hard to ensure our corporation meets Wall Street's expectation for earnings and performance (which continue to get more aggressive each year). In some cases, we run hard just to keep our job (a noble cause, by the way!). We run hard because, as a recent commercial says, "life comes at you fast."

This trend has worsened drastically in the last 10-15 years, and seems destined to accelerate in the years ahead. And, if unbridled, the lack of balance will have profound impacts on our physical, mental, and emotional health. In fact, it negatively impacts our effectiveness in all aspects of our lives—relationships (perhaps most significantly in our relationship with God), parenting, and work-related productivity, all of which will significantly impact the welfare of our marriages and our families.

Our culture encourages us to believe that with more hard work, we can accomplish anything. In truth, we can't. The Bible has a contrasting perspective on that notion in Proverbs 19:21: *Many are the plans in a man's heart, but it is the Lord's purpose that prevails.* You can work hard and have the best laid plans, but God is in control and we are not. Why, then, do we insist on running at "break neck" speed?

Consider these compelling work/life balance (or lack thereof) facts: [26]

- 40 percent of the U.S. workforce (and 46 percent of men) work between 40-60 hours per week.
- 33 percent of U.S. workers do some work-related activities every day of the week and 62% of workers have their personal lives interrupted by work at least 10 times per week.
- 63 percent of people asked in a recent survey said that they are "stressed out" and out of balance and more than half add that it has become worse in the last five years.
- The Journal of Occupational & Environmental Medicine reports that 38 percent of workers have experienced lack of sleep and fatigue in the previous two weeks. In fact, these same workers lose nearly six hours of work productivity each week as a result, costing U.S. businesses in excess of $100 billion in lost productivity annually.[27]

It's easy to be convinced this is a pervasive problem. The question becomes: how do we get control and create the balance that we not only crave but so badly need.

Achieving work/life balance

To create a better balance in our lives requires diligence, hard work, and intestinal fortitude. This is no panacea; there's no silver bullet here. But it's certainly worth some effort because progress allows us to be in alignment with God's will for us by having some semblance of order in our lives. We're far more likely to have a sense of purpose in life if we aren't spread too thin, always on the go, and consumed by life's barrage of activities.

I'll admit that in all the years I was working too many hours to "succeed," I would have said, with conviction, that I was a faithful Christian with a strong relationship with Jesus and that my life was as "centered" as the next business professional. And I honestly believed that was the case until one day in a hotel room in Tokyo, Japan.

I had just arrived in Japan after flying all of the previous day from Atlanta. It was 8:00am in Tokyo and my meeting was scheduled to begin at 9:00 am. I called home to see how the day had gone for Devonie and our three daughters (it was 8:00 pm Atlanta time and they were settled-in for the evening). We had a nice 10-15 minute conversation – much like other conversations we'd had over many years of my work and travel. The only difference this time was that when I hung up the phone I began to cry. Perhaps better described, I began to openly sob. I was filled with questions, "What was I doing thousands of miles away from my precious family, preparing to attend a meeting I cared little about? Is this where I belonged? If so, for what purpose - to make my firm more successful? How much should that matter relative to my priorities as a father and as a husband?"

It was a decisive moment for me because I began to fundamentally question my current career, my priorities, and my obvious lack of balance. I left Andersen Consulting within a year of that trip.

It wasn't the only (or last) time I struggled with these issues and I subsequently took on time-demanding roles in other organizations. But it was life-changing nonetheless. It's been more than six years since I left my last "traditional" corporate role in order to be more balanced and to do more of what God has called me (and made me) to do and the journey has given me a new perspective.

Foremost, I've learned what it means to have a personal relationship with Jesus, and it's not a part-time thing. I'm learning not to compartmentalize God into the Sunday morning "box." I've been proactively and consistently making the time to spend the first part of every day with God—in my favorite chair in my home office where it is quiet, comfortable, and relaxed. It's where I can read the Bible, talk to Him (either in prayer or through journaling) about what's going on in my life and in my heart, and to more fully discern what He wants me to understand. And there's plenty He wants me to better understand!

God is now an *integral* part of my life's journey, not a distant Creator I call on periodically as needs arise. I'm also learning to give up control of my life and my time to Him. He wants responsibility for the outcomes anyway. If I want God's help to create balance in my life, or to help me achieve a goal for that matter, why wouldn't I make sure to start each day—or each week, or each year—by asking Him what He would have me do?

Through balance, I'm also learning the techniques and the benefits of having the time and energy to do those things that are in alignment with my own skills and interests and to cut back on those things that aren't. It's liberating to feel a genuine sense of peace and, along with it, joy—about today and the future. Life is simpler today than it was six years ago—less pressure, fewer bills to pay (we've reduced our expenses by 30 percent), fewer things to maintain, and more time with the people I love most.

~ Balance is about being centered...on Christ! ~

In essence, balance is about being centered. Centered on Christ that is. Think of a teeter-totter you used to play on at the local park. Being on either end of the teeter-totter plank has lots of ups and downs (and bumps and bruises if you're not careful). If you're sitting at or near the center of the board – the ride is much smoother. Similarly, centering yourself on Christ is the starting point for creating work and life balance in our fast-paced world.

Keys to success

Here are some of the most important lessons gleaned from personal experience and from the lessons of others who have created a healthier work/life balance:

Daily prayer and quiet time with God. At the risk of being repetitive, it's the best and only way to start (or end) each day. Sometimes we think we're too busy to pray. That's about as senseless as saying we're too busy to breathe or eat. We're too busy *not* to pray! If we keep our perspective on our purpose and our destiny and recognize that God is in control, we'll allocate our time every day with the Savior who gave us life and the promise of an eternal future with Him in heaven. Be still and know that He is God.

Establish priorities. What's important to you, and does your current investment of time and energy align with your priorities? We all tend to fall victim to the activity trap. We often react to requests and needs that present themselves, and we have few filters to help us decide what's worth our time. Life is all about tradeoffs and we can't do it all. The challenge is to determine proactively what criteria we should use to choose the right activities and say "no" to others.

Remember the calendar alignment exercise we discussed in the last chapter? How does your calendar line up with your priorities? You may be surprised—and disappointed, if you do it honestly. Though most Christians would rank God, spouse, children, and work as very high on the list, when we examine the time we give to each priority, the reality of our behavior is often in reverse order.

That doesn't mean you have the luxury of deciding that you're not going to spend much time working because it's only number five on the list. With that strategy, you may end up with lots of free time (and no job). But it does serve as a challenge to create a criteria filter that allows you to proactively say "yes" and "no" as you allocate your precious time. Break the tendency of simply being reactive to the next request or event. With a "permission" system based on proactively choosing your priorities, you'll improve your ability to say "yes" to the right activities and ensure that it happens.

~ Does your calendar align with your priorities? ~

Here's a simple example to illustrate the power of the approach: It's Thursday afternoon, and a work colleague invites you to go to the baseball game that evening with a couple of other friends. It's August—the middle of the pennant race—and it should be a great game. Do you say yes or no? The easy choice is to go to the game. But that may ignore your priorities (depending on whether baseball and this friend are near the top of your list of priorities). Your other choice is to spend that same time on your chosen priorities: like taking your wife out to dinner, spending the evening helping your kids with a project, or playing family games. Priority based decisions.

Schedule priorities first. The best way to ensure progress on your most critical priorities, either personally or professionally, is to put them on your calendar in advance, before other distractions can get in the way. For example, when Devonie and I have been running hard and want to get re-connected by having lunch together, we put it on both of our calendars and it becomes an event that we then schedule around. I do the same for my daily quiet time, for my exercise, and for my career ministry work. I sometimes even schedule "planning time," which allows me to do the "not urgent, but important" priorities that we covered in the last chapter. If I don't, those precious time slots become consumed with the issue du jour, and I become a victim of activities again. Use this philosophy as you plan your days, your weeks, and your months. Become intentional about your priorities and your precious time.

Don't add without subtracting. Andy Stanley, senior pastor at our church, Northpoint Community Church in Alpharetta, Georgia gets credit for this adage. His point is that we often act as though we have unlimited time and can say yes to everything that comes along, particularly if we have a few free minutes on an otherwise packed calendar. The reality is that our time is finite, and we may or may not have much "extra" time if we don't manage it effectively. Get in the habit of subtracting something from your calendar whenever you add an activity or a priority. An example: A friend asks you to help deliver "meals on wheels" once a week to elderly people in the community. Instead of imme-diately agreeing, carefully consider what activity you'll *stop* doing to accommodate this request. Maybe you decide you'll no longer be your son's room mother this year, depending on where this fits in the scheme of your family priorities. As you can see, it's important to have a pre-determined "permission" system to decide on these kinds of invitations and activities.

Just say "no." You can't do it all, and it's critical to resist the temptation to try. I know firsthand how hard it is to say "no" to the worthwhile requests you get, particularly when you have nothing previously committed for that time on your calendar. But remember that the important things in life often happen in the margins of life — not during furious daily activities. It's when things are quiet at your house and your teenage son finally decides, because it's quiet and a "safe" environment, to ask your advice about how to deal with a friend who's getting into drugs and inviting him to join the crowd. Unless you preserve the margin in you and your family's life, you'll never know you missed this discussion until your son starts exhibiting the behaviors of a teenager struggling with an addiction—or worse.

Create boundaries. To help enable your priorities to dictate your choices, establish some boundaries. A friend we'll call "Mark" told me about boundaries he and his wife established after she became completely exhausted with his work, his travel, and his neglect of their family as he ran the North American division of a large manufacturer. Without boundaries, he was dangerously close to losing his family. Simple examples of boundaries he shared with me:

- "I won't work past 6 p.m. on any weekday to preserve evening time with my family."
- "I won't travel overnight for more than eight nights per month."
- "I'll turn off my Blackberry at 7:00 pm every evening."

~ Establish boundaries that keep the right things in and the wrong things out ~

Once you determine these boundaries you've got to be resolute in upholding them – which may be the hardest part of the equation. What will you define as your boundaries? Choose your own - just make sure you have some.

Create "margin" in your work. I know, it's easier said than done. Allow me to argue with your first reaction, though. I believe one major reason we have too little professional margin is that our pride gets in the way. We want to believe, and want others to believe, that we're capable of doing more than the average human can accomplish. It's just our nature. In reality, most of us possess two or three core competencies, and much of the rest of our work is not in our "sweet spot."

The best technique for creating margin at work is to determine the intersection between the functions and tasks most emphasized in your job description and the skills that represent your core competencies, and then to spend the majority of your time on these. In other words, play to your strengths and spend little (or no) time on the less valuable functions that are often your weaknesses. If you don't employ this strategy, you'll attempt to do everything and likely end up with mediocre results. It may take time to adjust your job focus to fit your key skills, but once you do, your employer will get more value and you'll have more margin in your life.

Be bold enough to make changes. If you have a job that makes unreasonable demands on your time and energy and doesn't allow you alignment with your priorities in life, be faithful enough to make a career change. Three separate times in my career I resolved to change in favor of better balance and alignment, and, in retrospect, I'm utterly amazed at how carefully God has orchestrated the process and the outcome. Too often, our lack of faith in God's almighty power prevents us from doing the right things (and the hard things, like leaving an untenable work situation). You'll benefit from collaborating with your spouse and/or a trusted friend in evaluating and making these tough choices. Just don't be too busy or faithless to make the changes you decide are right for you and your family.

Creating work/life balance isn't easy, particularly in today's culture and work environment. People like me, who God has filled with high doses of passion and an extra helping of Type A personality, have a lifelong struggle in this area. But I'm convinced that the obedient thing for working people to do is to ensure that you have alignment between your work, your life, your time, and your spiritual priorities. And that's what work/life balance is all about – being "centered" on Christ in all that we do.

Chapter 7 Reflection Questions

- Do you think you have a healthy work/life balance right now? Why or why not?
- What are the biggest challenges you face to gain or maintain balance?
- What is most negatively impacted by your lack of balance: Your health? Your marriage? Your family? Your job? Your relationship with God? Or something else?
- Is there any correlation between your satisfaction in these areas and the time and energy you currently devote to them?
- What specific steps can you commit to take to improve your work/life balance?

Section III

The <u>Maps</u>: Flourishing in the New World of Work

—ᗰ—

Most people want to know how to survive in the new world of work. But why be satisfied with simply surviving? God has far better for us than mere survival. He wants us to flourish! In this section, we'll focus on just that.

We've already established that the ground rules of work have changed and these changes in the work environment are here to stay, perhaps they'll even accelerate. The following chapters will help equip you to take practical steps to succeed in this new environment. If you decide you're not currently doing work that takes best advantage of your God-given gifts and passions, let's explore how you can gain the right skills, get exposed to the right opportunities, and find the best options. If you determine that you're in the right work but something else is missing, we'll explore how to best leverage your current environment. Flourishing has a lot to do with your mindset and throughout this section we'll outline the key dimensions critical to your success.

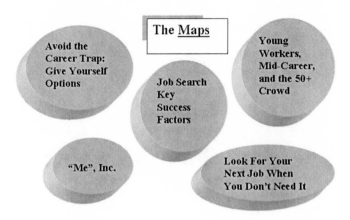

~ No Longer Dominated by Work:
Phil and Barbara Johnson ~

Phil is relaxed and unstructured. Barb is budget-conscious and well-organized. Though they both grew up in Atlanta, Phil is an Auburn grad with an MBA from Georgia State; Barb earned a degree at the University of Georgia. (In the south, we consider this a "mixed marriage.") Apparently, opposites really do attract.

Phil worked hard in high school and nearly full-time during college. He worked as a management trainee at a cafeteria, managed apartment leasing, and became an auditor for a school district, often while running his own yard maintenance business as a second job. Then Phil joined a software company called McCormack and Dodge and held a variety of jobs, including consulting services, sales and sales management, and marketing. He worked hard and traveled often.

When Phil obtained custody of his 12-year-old son from his first marriage, he realized he'd have to find a new way to make a living that allowed him both the stability and flexibility to take on this new responsibility. As a result, he shifted his career to the sales training business, where he has been an instructor for two different companies over the past 15 years. His skills and his passion for teaching have made this an ideal career and he has achieved the balance in his life that he didn't enjoy in traditional corporate positions.

Barb, on the other hand, calls herself an overachiever. She began her career straight out of college with a software company called Management Science America (MSA), where she moved from product development to account management, to ultimately being responsible for managing worldwide services. When MSA merged with McCormack and Dodge, Phil and Barbara met and eventually "merged" (married) in 1991. Barb, in the interest of lifestyle goals—less travel, less intense work environment, more work-life balance—eventually worked for three different companies after MSA, most recently as a contract employee in the North Atlanta area where she and Phil now live.

Visiting with Phil and Barbara, you quickly notice the contrast in personalities. Phil is relaxed, not much of a worrier, and a self-professed golf fanatic. Barb, on the other hand, is the organizer, the one concerned with handling the money, scheduling the family's activities, and managing projects skillfully. Over time, they have determined how to make the best of their skills and talents.

"In 1992, when we took custody of Phil Jr., our priorities really changed," explained Phil. He and Barb agreed that for many years their personal motivations had centered on their careers and their ability to make and save money. Work had dominated their lives. Coming to that awareness was the beginning of several milestones that were instrumental in their journey to finding deeper fulfillment and peace in their lives.

A second milestone came in 1997 when they started going back to church and recommitted to studying God's

Word. "We began to see that there was more to life than work," says Barb. "I knew I had many talents that had been applied to a work environment but found that they were equally valuable in a church and charitable environment."

That same year, they also began to plan for their future. Even though Barb was reducing her work commitments and therefore making less money, they began to manage their budget more strictly and save half of Barb's income, with the goal of buying their dream house on a lake within a few years. They eventually saved enough to acquire some lakefront property in North Georgia and subsequently built the home they reside in today and to which they plan to retire.

Barb reflected on their financial and life decisions: "As our income has gone down, it seems that our happiness has gone up." Their only debt is their home mortgage, and they are frugal spenders—they drive "mature" cars and spend little on clothes and entertainment. "In the past several years," adds Phil, "we've really begun to trust God and let go."

They've also had their share of trials. A few years ago, Barb was diagnosed with cancer and was successfully treated back to full health. It was another example of a setback that the couple has faced, dealt with, and trusted God to help them overcome. She says, "Life's too short to worry about the little things."

Lessons Learned

Phil: "Either do what you love, or love what you do; choosing anything else is counterproductive."

Barb: "The marriage relationship is key. You've got to learn to communicate about difficult issues and decisions and to trust each other."

They both agreed that it's important to be flexible as unplanned circumstances arise. Whether it's taking custody of a child, a layoff at work, or even the onset of cancer, we all have priorities to assess and choices to make. Those who are able to make hard and prudent choices can adapt to anything that comes their way.

Chapter 8

Me, Inc.

—~~—

The changing relationship between employers and employees has profound implications for you and your career. Above all, it requires a change in your self-perception from "company employee" to "free agent."

Among the more significant trends in this employment relationship is the declining level of commitment of employees to their employers. That loyalty will continue to drop as workers give much less emphasis to working for companies that provide a long-term career and pension, and far more emphasis to working for an organization that allows them to be challenged, to learn, and to broaden their experience.

Employer loyalty continues to drop as well. Corporations today rely less on full-time, long-term employees and rely increasingly on an employment model that gives them the best talent for a specific function for a specific time frame (often a pre-determined contract period to build a new capability or complete a project, for example). This model allows the corporation to maximize the flexibility in their cost structure, minimize hiring and severance costs, and minimizes "fixed" costs, which Wall Street always appreciates and rewards.

I've spent much of the last five years coaching and supporting many unemployed and employed workers who are in career transition for a variety of reasons (fired, laid off, or just decided to make a change). While the traditional, full-time/permanent option is usually the career seeker's preference, workers today are wise to consider less traditional alternatives. That could mean becoming an independent contractor or a temp, or even changing career paths entirely.

In order to do that, it will be necessary to dispense with some of our current paradigms. Contrary to common belief, for example, contract and temp workers are not limited to clerical and industrial jobs. In fact, the Bureau of Labor Statistics data shows that technical and professional jobs (including computer programmers, managers, executives, and financial-services professionals) are among the fastest-growing occupational categories in the temporary staffing industry.

Human resource professionals are another example that reflects this change in the market. This job function has been caught in the "perfect storm" and it's been among the toughest job categories in recent years. Corporations have continued to find creative ways to automate previously labor-intensive HR functions (payroll, health care benefits, pension plans, etc.) via web-based enrollment and management tools. As a result, thousands of HR professionals have been victims of the corporate downsizing that tends to follow these productivity improvements. There simply are not as many HR positions available as there once were, particularly at the same level and pay. These workers have at least four practical options:

- Patiently wait for an opportunity to replace the job they left – which may take more time than they can afford to wait.

- Take a lower-level (and lower-paying) position in HR—perhaps even entry-level.
- Look for an entirely new career path that leverages their skills and interests.
- Look for alternative employment arrangements (part time, job sharing, project based, etc.).

These trends are not simply a corporation-driven phenomenon. American workers themselves have also decided in ever-increasing numbers that they would rather be free agents. Some estimate that these free agents will represent one-third of the workforce by 2010. The trend is pervasive because people desire more control of their destiny. Most workers want more control and better balance between their career and the rest of life.

One way to accomplish these goals is to embrace a new paradigm about your employment: from that of being an employee of one organization; to contributing your core skills to one or more organizations simultaneously. Think of yourself as "Me," Inc.—i.e.. Paul, Inc.; Mary, Inc.; Anybody, Inc.!

~ Think "Me," Inc. ~

This shift in attitude requires you to stop thinking of yourself as a small, unimportant employee of a large, important organization. Instead, begin carrying the confidence that you are a valuable entity in and of yourself and you provide your skills and experience to a business (or businesses) that can benefit from them. Stop thinking of yourself and your career as a small cog in a huge gear system. For as long as you do, you'll tend to assume that someone else is responsible for your career, your personal development, and even your well-being. Your career destiny then becomes largely dictated by others.

Part of the reason this mindset shift is required is that long job tenure for most is a thing of the past. Remember - the average person graduating from college this year is likely to have more than 13 jobs in their career. That's an average of roughly three years for each job. When you find a new job, you can hope that it will last for 10+ years but the likelihood is that it will last a much shorter time period. Many of us will be commonly looking for new work – which is a great reason to embrace this new career mindset – Me, Inc.

Marketing your product: You

Think of it like this: *you* are a product—a valuable, marketable product that has many capabilities and can be utilized for many different functions, potentially in a variety of companies. You are an entrepreneur responsible for the success of this product called Me, Inc., and your job is to optimize the five P's of marketing: Product, Packaging, Promotion, Price, and Place—all of which are grounded in your overall strategy of how to maximize your success.

- Investing in your **Product**—you'll want to ensure that your product has the best capabilities, the best features, the most marketable skills, and the most knowledge to accomplish the goals you aspire to achieve. This will require your time, your energy, and in many cases your personal investment in training and development. Personal development won't happen overnight; it will likely involve a lifetime commitment.
- **Packaging** your product—you'll want to make certain that your product (you, of course) is well understood by the available market (potential employers). You'll do this by ensuring that your "features," your "benefits," and your "fit" are clearly defined and that

A Better Way to Make a Living ...and a Life

the market recognizes how and where you can best contribute.

- **Promotion** and sales—you'll also take responsibility for publicizing your capabilities to ensure that potential employers know who you are and how to find you if they need your skills. To succeed, you must become adept at clearly stating your value, your unique capabilities, and your commitment to serve your clients. You'll need testimonials from organizations that have experienced the benefits of your product to share with other companies that might also benefit. Many people struggle with this because it isn't comfortable for most of us to brag about ourselves. You'll have to get over it. Promotion will also likely require you to develop strong networking skills to help identify opportunities (more on that in Chapter 11).

- **Price**—with the Me, Inc. mindset, you'll also have a good sense of your worth in the job market and what companies are willing to pay people with similar skills and attributes. And your product's value is likely greater (at least in terms of dollars per hour) to a company as a part time or contract employee than it would be for a more traditional "permanent" employee.

- **Place**—where is your product available and how can an employer buy some or all of your available time? Your physical presence may be needed at the company you are working for, but it's increasingly possible to deliver your knowledge and skills on a somewhat "virtual" basis, largely because of advances in communications, the Internet, and related collaboration tools.

Remember, each of these dimensions applies equally to the worker who is working full time for one employer as

169

it does to the person who chooses to leverage their skills across more than one company. It simply represents a new paradigm for all of us.

You "own" your career

Too many workers feel as though someone other than themselves is responsible for what happens in their career. Most are sadly disappointed, though, about the degree that others (including your employers) care about your future. Some workers are fortunate enough to have a genuinely caring manager who shows a sincere interest in their advancement and personal development, but those managers are the exception, not the rule. The reality today is that we all need to take ownership of our own career – both present and future.

I recall visiting with Harold a couple of years ago when he was between assignments. He's an IT professional who got tired of working for organizations that would hire him and then, a few months later, decide they no longer needed his help. He was being hired and managed as a temporary employee of sorts without any of the advantages. So he developed a strategy: "I decided I was better off focusing my efforts on becoming an IT contractor and began marketing myself through multiple IT contracting organizations. Now I have control over who I work for and how long I accept an assignment, and I'm less dependent on any one employer for my livelihood. And, I make an income premium of 30 percent more per hour for being a contract resource than I would make as a 'permanent' employee."

Harold began navigating his own career journey. Who's going to navigate in your career journey? When I use terms like "take ownership," "take control," or "navigate your journey," I'm obviously not referring to having a spirit of independence about being in charge of your own plans without regard for God's will. What I mean is having the freedom to pursue the directions God has called you into without being compromised or stifled by employer expectations or feeling stuck in the status quo. Too many people allow their career to be guided by a company or a work culture rather than proactively seeking God's will and maintaining the freedom to follow it.

In the first 10 years of my career, I can remember a couple of instances when I felt I wasn't being treated fairly by my employer—perhaps disappointed that I wasn't considered for a key promotion, or that my pay increase wasn't adequate. It was easy to feel like a victim. Easy, that is, until I realized that nobody cares as much about my career and my success as I do. I went from the passive approach ("I hope they have my best interests at heart") to the proactive approach ("I need to help make things happen"). That doesn't mean you can force things to happen or that God isn't ultimately guiding your career and life. And we're still required to be the best contributors we can possibly be in any role assigned to us. In fact, excellent work gives us the confidence and credibility to enable us to be proactive.

One big leap I made personally was when a friend of mine, Bill Morganstern, challenged me to give myself "permission" to *not* think about myself as an employee, which I spent most of my career doing. Bill, who specializes in helping executives work through career transition issues (finding new work, starting a new business, transitioning to retirement, etc.), instead encouraged me to consider alternative career paths—including my current career in the sales training and consulting business.

When I initially joined The Complex Sale in 1998, it was the first job I'd ever had that didn't pay me a salary. On one hand, that can be downright scary. On the other, I've learned that with this arrangement I can work as hard as I choose to in order to meet the personal and professional goals I've established. If my goal is to make a high income—then I'll put in the time and effort to achieve these goals. On the other hand, when I reach the point where I want to spend more time on my other projects and avocations (like Crossroads Career Network, writing, or something else), I have the flexibility to make these personal choices, and I'll be satisfied to earn less money. That's the liberating part of this type of arrangement.

~ You're not "just" an employee! ~

It was hard to make this transition at first because I had, for so many years, become accustomed to a steady, predictable paycheck that was directly deposited into my checking account every two weeks, no matter what. It was a major source of security for me. What I've learned about myself in the last few years is that my current "highly leveraged" role (i.e., no salary) suits me extraordinarily well because I don't feel the sense of duty associated with a salaried position that drives my workaholic tendencies. I've said to Devonie on many occasions, "If my employer is going to pay me well to do this job, I want them to get their money's worth." It's the way God built me—for better or for worse. A no-salary position takes that dynamic out of the equation.

How can you take more control with a Me, Inc. approach? It doesn't mean you have to leave the employer you're currently with. You may very well continue full-time with one employer. It does mean, however, that you take more ownership for the valuable asset you represent to your current employer or others. Your gifts and talents are not an accident, and your career shouldn't be accidental either.

This Me, Inc model won't suit everyone. It requires a person to sell him/herself more than some are comfortable with doing. And it requires a shift in your mindset.

The paradigm shift

To begin to adjust to a Me, Inc. attitude requires the following paradigm shifts:

Shift From:	Shift To:
"I'm an employee and always will be."	"I have a great opportunity to leverage my skills in multiple environments, perhaps even simultaneously, as an employee or perhaps as a contractor. It might be full time, or better yet, part time, where I have the flexibility to work for more than one company at the same time. This may be ideal for me (variety, less dependence on any one company and its success, or lack thereof), but is also beneficial to those who employ my skills."
"I'll do whatever it takes to pay my bills, even if it's not a great fit for my skills and interests."	"I was designed by God with very specific talents and gifts. These were not an accident, nor should my career be accidental. Even if today I'm in a role that is not an ideal (or even a close) fit, my goal is to find the role that is consistent with and takes advantage of my God-given talents. This may take time and effort, but it honors God to find the role that allows my light (and skills) to shine for others to see and benefit from."

"I expect to have this job indefinitely (i.e. forever)."	"I expect that the role I currently occupy is for the short/mid-term, and the prudent thing for me to do is to consistently explore other career options and alternatives in order to maximize my opportunities—both short and long-term. This is not being dis-loyal or underhanded to my current employer! It's simply recognition that there is no longer permanence in today's job market, and both employer and employee are best served to understand this reality."
"I will do what's best for my employer, no matter the cost to me personally, to my family, or to my career."	"I must do what's best for Me, Inc. *and* ensure that my client (the company I work for) gets fair value for fair compensation. If either of these doesn't occur, the relationship will likely be short-lived."
"My employer is responsible for my career development."	"No one will care for my career and my future like I will, so I'll take personal responsibility for my development, including training. To whatever extent my employer can contribute, so much the better!"

"I feel dependent on my employer for my well-being and future."	"I am clearly benefiting from my current employer relationship, but I'm not relying on it to take care of my long-term career. I'm proactively exploring career options; I'm exploring options to create health insurance plans that reduce my reliance on any single employer; and I'm increasingly recognizing that my long term well-being is far better placed in the care of my Heavenly Father—for now and eternity."
"I'll keep doing this job until the next one comes along."	"I'll continue to do an exceptional job in my current role, but I will continuously and actively identify and pursue new opportunities simultaneously for the benefit of all concerned."
"I don't have time to network with people outside of my day-to-day responsibilities."	"I must proactively network with other people, inside and outside of my direct contacts, in order to nurture existing relationships and develop new ones for the benefit of discovering future opportunities and serving the needs of others in the process."

"Since I'm more than 50 years old, I'm just happy to have a job at all"	"Because I'm over 50, I have exceptional skills and experiences. I'm willing to minimize the risk for the employer who is concerned with my energy, health, or my likelihood of retiring prematurely by working on a contract or part-time basis. I will be comfortable, perhaps even eager, for alternative work arrangements that are good for me and good for my employer."

It's obvious from these contrasts that this will not be a natural shift for many because it runs so counter to the way we've been taught to think. This shift would not have been needed if the employment environment hadn't changed dramatically, but it has. It's imperative for workers to adapt accordingly.

Benefits of Me, Inc.

Why does this attitude shift make sense? Here are a few reasons discovered by many others who have taken advantage of this career route:

- Even if you're working entirely for one company, a Me, Inc. attitude gives you the distinct advantage (and peace associated with) being in control of your own career destiny. You are responsible for your future, your career direction, and the investments you make to improve your asset (you).
- If, on the other hand, you're working with more than one company, it reduces your dependency on any one organization's business conditions. If any single

client only represents one-half or one-third of your income, your risks are substantially reduced, particularly if your clients are in diverse industries.

- You'll likely increase your income potential because your value to multiple organizations in need of your specialty is greater than it is to a single organization. Usually, the rate you can charge is also higher than you would earn on an equivalent salary basis, particularly if you provide your own health benefits.
- It also provides you a level of independence and flexibility that few full-time employees enjoy. You have the liberty to choose the work that suits you, to work with the clients you want to work with, and flexibility to take time off—when you want or need it, not at the whim of others.

Genuine humility

The Me, Inc. mindset is not synonymous with either pride or arrogance. In fact, with a biblical perspective on our work, this mindset is actually entirely compatible with God's desire for our genuine humility. Paul admonishes us all in Philippians 2:3, *Do nothing out of selfish ambition or vain conceit, but in humility consider others better than yourselves.* This is not about feeling superior or more valuable than other people (or your employer for that matter). It *is* very much about aspiring to best utilize your gifts and talents in the greatest ways possible, for common good, and for God's ultimate glory. Perhaps a bit more encouragement comes from Proverbs 22:4, *Humility and the fear of the Lord bring wealth and honor and life.*

Final Thought:

It's time to recognize that the employment dynamics are changing, and those who can make the Me, Inc. shift will be more valuable, more marketable, more confident, and will ultimately fare better, both short- and long-term. Instead of becoming intimidated or frustrated by these trends—regardless of whether you're employed full time, part-time, or even unemployed—become proactive in considering how to take advantage of these trends and the opportunities that a Me, Inc. mentality can represent.

Chapter 8 Reflection Questions:

- How would you describe your current mindset about your job and career—as an employee or as Me, Inc.? Why?
- What practical steps can you take to begin to manage your career in a Me, Inc. fashion? How much of a mental shift would this require for you?
- What do you see as the risks and/or rewards of doing so? How, specifically, might a Me, Inc. perspective help your career?
- Do you know others who have this mindset? What can you learn from the way they have approached their work/career?

Chapter 9

Avoid the Career Trap: Give Yourself Options

—⁓—

Have you ever felt trapped in a less-than-satisfying job? Most of us have. And then often convince ourselves, with excuses like these, that we have no choice:

- "I can't leave this job because I've got bills to pay."
- "I'm not qualified to do anything else, so I'm stuck where I am."
- "My spouse and I are both going to be working until we can't work any more because we're accustomed to our joint income."
- "If I try to change careers, it will take too long to make the same money I make today. It's impossible!"
- "I don't have time to look for a new or better job. I'm too busy."

A few years ago I sat down with a friend who had been laid off from his job as Chief Financial Officer for a local company. We met to brainstorm about his career options. He wasn't particularly satisfied with his previous role or even with the finance career he had pursued in the first place. But he felt stuck, "I have to find another job that pays $150,000, so I have no choice about my career options."

"Can you reduce your current expenses to give yourself more options?" I asked.

His immediate response was typical: "You don't understand. My kids love their private school, my wife has become accustomed to not working, and the whole family loves the new house we moved into last year."

One of the worst afflictions any of us can have is the perception that you are stuck and have no choices—especially related to our careers. We all have choices! If you're feeling trapped in your current job or career, the best gift you can give yourself is to increase your options. Wouldn't you feel a sense of liberation—or better yet, a sense of peace and gratification—if you could honestly say, "I have three other paths to consider if my current career plan doesn't work out—and they all provide sufficient income and match well with my skills and interests?" It's amazing how few people can actually make that statement.

~ Do your current income (or expenses) limit your career options? ~

The goal is simple: to be able to choose the work you do, who you work for, and even how much you work. The epitome of this flexibility is the wealthy person who has unlimited options—including the option of not working at all. While that's a nice aspiration, it's a life most of us won't soon experience. The other extreme might be to live with your parents for the rest of your life, never marry or have kids, and contain your expenses so well that you don't need to work much, or even at all. For most of us, this option is possible but far from appealing.

So the challenge is to operate somewhere between these two extremes in a way that releases us from a feeling of serving a life sentence of hard labor. Feeling trapped by your current obligations, financial or otherwise, is unnecessary. God's design for our work and life is better than that.

The culprits

The most prevalent reasons that the average worker feels trapped in their current job or career generally falls into one of a few categories:

- We're either too busy or too complacent (or lazy?) to look for better options. The easiest path, the path of least resistance, is to do nothing. It's human nature. We get so busy with life that we aren't proactive about finding reasonable alternatives. I've met countless people who complain about their current situation and, when I ask them what they're doing about it, they usually answer "nothing." And as long as we're satisfied with a miserable and/or unfulfilling job, we'll continue to do nothing. To me, this seems a lot like the person who foolishly argues, "I'm too busy to get better organized!"
- Some actually feel trapped because they make more money in a job than they are likely to make with other options. Examples include the doctor who hates the nature of her practice but makes so much money that she rules out alternatives; or the consultant who enjoys making 50 percent more than his college fraternity brothers, though he's traveling 80 percent of the time and rarely spends quality time with his family. The pay, the pride, or maybe the challenge and personal affirmations of this career make it hard for him to step down.

- Other workers determine that they don't have the necessary skills for a more attractive career. They've been trained in one discipline and conclude they don't have the time and/or the money to be trained for what they feel most gifted to do.

- Perhaps most commonly, many have allowed their expenses to grow at a rate as fast, or faster, than their income and they can't consider career options because they can't afford the risk of falling behind financially. This can happen to families making a household income of $100,000 per year or more as easily as to one making $50,000. Of course, people often view their expenses as "fixed" as opposed to "variable"— and they make the false assumption that few, if any, of their costs can be eliminated. An example is the couple that "has to" make $90,000 per year just to pay the bills, which may include extraordinary credit card debt or the all-important monthly country club dues (that they can't afford).

Maximizing options

There are very few good reasons to feel trapped in your current work, especially if you're dissatisfied with your position. The Bible gives us a liberating promise for work and life: *"I know the plans I have for you," declares the Lord, "plans to prosper you and not to harm you, plans to give you hope and a future"* (Jeremiah 29:11). What more could we ask for from the Creator of work Himself?

This biblical promise provides reassurance that God doesn't expect or want you to view your work as a life sentence. If you're feeling trapped in today's job, here are some suggestions designed to ensure that you increase your career options:

Fight complacency: You can't afford to become so complacent that you assume there are no alternatives. Yes, exploring options requires effort. On the other hand, it can actually be the most energizing thing to do for yourself because focusing on finding the work God has designed especially for you can fill you with enthusiasm about your future. In essence it provides hope. And without hope, people see no end to their plight. Being proactive will give you a real sense of hope for something better that we all desire.

Learn new skills: The more you know, the more skills you possess, and the more diversified your experience, the more options you'll have in your career—and in life, for that matter. Some of these skills are gained in on-the-job situations. It's why young workers are wise to get a diverse set of experiences in the first five years of their career, even within the same organization. That could mean a stint in finance, then operations, and then a sales role, for example. That allows you to gain excellent experience while sorting out what you really enjoy and what you're good at doing. The young person who spends the first 10 years of his or her career in one function, like accounts payable, is often disadvantaged because potential employers then judge that person as being one-dimensional.

For many, diversity of experience can also come in the form of extracurricular activities. The key is to determine where your interests and passions lie. Is it photography? Developing websites? Scrapbooking?[28] A new language? Or something else? These and a slew of other interests have led many to shift their careers in mid-life because they developed a new talent, and often a new passion. Resist the excuse that you don't have time. You have the time to develop these interests and skills; you simply have to make them a priority.

Be patient and have confidence: Believe this truth: when people commit to pursue work that they are most gifted to do, they will do it so well that someone or some company is more than willing to pay them well to do it. You may not start off replacing your previous income, but with time, patience, and diligence you will be rewarded for your efforts.

Don't spend to your income level: This may be the hardest (and most important) thing for most of us to do because, for a variety of reasons, we tend to have our next pay increase spent before it even hits our bank account. Or worse yet, we accumulate debt to the point that we can't even pay our current expenses with our current income. We're all far better off setting a goal to live on less than we make. For example, can you learn to control your expenses enough to live on 60 percent of your net (take-home) pay? If not, what about 70 percent? Making this work requires a simpler set of lifestyle choices. Here are a few obvious examples:

- a modest house instead of a large, luxurious one
- buying used cars instead of new; or keeping new ones for 7-10 years instead of 3-4 years like so many do
- shopping for clothes at Marshall's or Ross instead of Nordstrom's
- driving vacations to campgrounds instead of flying to the Bahamas (the kids are likely to enjoy camping more anyway)
- a state university for the kids' education instead of a private college

I think you get the idea. One of my favorite principles related to this is to spend on "needs" and save for "wants." The hard part is knowing the difference because we all have personal definitions for needs versus wants. But the principle is sound.

The most powerful part of these strategies is that those who reduce their spending successfully will benefit from having many more options in their career and in their lives. As you read the stories I have included in this book, you'll notice the trend: people able to live where they want, do the work they find most fulfilling, and in many cases pursue their passions because they don't feel trapped by their current expenses. Here are a few additional benefits of living on a smaller portion of your net pay:

- Helps you save and invest for the future (which can create "passive" income).
- Helps to be more generous with God-given resources—tithing, for example.
- Helps deal with unplanned expenses without living on the edge of financial crisis.
- And, it's almost certain to improve your ability to sleep at night!

~ Spend on needs. Save for wants. The hard part: knowing the difference ~

It's probably easier for a young person to adopt this philosophy and discipline from the start of their career. And yet, mid-career couples can embrace the approach as well. Yes, it'll be tough to make some changes if you're already in a set of spending habits. But why not try to gain some peace of mind by gaining control of your spending?

Devonie and I faced the critical decision early in our marriage of whether she would continue to work once we began to have children—she became pregnant with our first child within ten months after our wedding. We were both working at the time, and I wasn't making enough money to support all of our expenses. As much as we wanted to have both incomes to get our family off to a good financial start, we also knew that if we became accustomed to a second income, it would be increasingly difficult to wean ourselves from it as the years passed. We also decided that one priority in raising our family was that Devonie would be able to be at home with the children.

Now Devonie has spent 25 years managing our household and loving and nurturing our children and, in the last two years, has gone back to work part time. She loves being able to contribute in a work environment, and she loves the flexibility she has with part-time work. As for our three daughters, they've all grown up to be gifted young women who have completed college and have all found the one thing we have most prayed for: a strong relationship with our Savior—praise God! The trade-off decisions we make are critical—and should be purpose and priority-based.

Let's look at one more perspective on money and stewardship of our resources—God's. Here are a few verses to consider:

- *No one can serve two masters...You cannot serve both God and money* (Matthew 6:24). The clarity of this verse is striking. He doesn't say we *might* not be able to serve both. He says we can't!
- *...for everything in heaven and earth is yours...* (1 Chronicles 29:11) The Lord is the owner of all things and we're called to be good stewards of financial resources - manage your money accordingly.
- *So if you have not been trustworthy in handling worldly wealth, who will trust you with true riches?"* (Luke 16:11) How we handle money impacts our relationship with God – are you faithful in your use of God's provision?
- *...the borrower is servant to the lender* (Proverbs 22:7) This verse best highlights the notion that being in debt is much like servitude – talk about having few options!

The point is obvious. As you consider your spending habits and your use of credit cards and debt, keep asking, "Is this what God would embrace or admonish?" And the wiser we are in this regard, the more flexibility you'll have in finding a better way to make a living...and a life.

Final Thought

Having career options is incredibly liberating, just ask anyone you know who experiences this "freedom." I pray that many more individuals and couples will be bold and brave enough to find proactive ways to give themselves more career options. Will you?

Chapter 9 Reflection questions:

- Do you feel trapped in your current job? Why? What limits your ability to change to something better suited to your skills and interests?
- What job and/or career options would you most like to pursue if you felt you had the option?
- What are the impediments to getting there: Training? Financial obligations? Lack of confidence?
- What steps can you take to reduce or eliminate these impediments? How can you ensure that your spouse/ family are supportive and aligned with these steps?

Chapter 10

Look For Your Next Job When You Don't Need It

—〰—

First and foremost, you'll be best-served in your career to excel in your current role at your current company. This will not only maximize your experience and track record but will also give you the very best opportunity to get promotions and pay increases exactly where you are.

At the same time, however, whether you're starting with a new company or have been with your current employer for many years, the changes in the employer/employee contract require a new paradigm about looking for alternatives. So on one hand we should contribute as much as possible to our current employer—a fair day's work for a fair day's pay. On the other hand, because both employer and employee have evolved to ensure that our respective best interests are a foremost priority in the relationship (which isn't a bad concept), we now have both the right and responsibility to keep our eyes open for new and better opportunities as they present themselves—or, perhaps better said, as we find them.

Maximizing the opportunities in your current company/job

Whether you're in the perfect job with a company that suits you well or in a tenuous work environment with a questionable future, there a few key pointers to enhance your career – right where you are today:

- *Exceed expectations.* This is the most important strategy in this entire chapter because it maximizes your value for both your current employer and potential future employers. Most people who are thinking about their next job tend to mentally check out of the one they're in. That's a mistake – performing with excellence will serve you well, no exceptions.
- *Develop your credibility and relationship with your manager.* Managers are often the critical relationship for your advancement and success within your current company—and they can also make your life miserable if they choose. Great and supportive managers also tend to be the first to recruit their most trusted and talented workers to the next company they go work for.
- *Learn as much as you can in your current role about your company, its customers, its products, and even its competitors.* This knowledge will make you a more effective employee where you are and a more valuable asset in the market. The more you know, the better.
- *Have a great and infectious attitude.* There are few things you can do to make real career progress than having a genuinely positive attitude (not just a happy face). It dramatically and positively impacts the perception of your current employer – managers and peers alike. It also becomes habitual – and any employer will value a great attitude.

- *Look for opportunities to glorify God with your actions, your ethics, and your service-oriented approach.* Few Christians really understand that their job is an opportunity, a platform for deeper matters than simply earning a living. The nature of your work matters to you quite a bit, but the nature of your work relationships is a much bigger issue in God's eyes. Perhaps your workplace "ministry" involves remaining calm in an otherwise stormy department or your ability to share your faith with others. Determine how to make your work your own personal mission field and the nature of the work itself will become secondary to your "primary" higher calling.

And yet, be diligent in looking for your next job

I know it sounds like heresy, but this is what prudent workers do, particularly those with a Me, Inc. attitude. A parallel is the evolution of professional athletes. Before the concept of free agency, baseball players were most often with a team for the majority (if not all) of their career. Today, both players and owners are pretty dispassionate in their willingness to trade a "franchise" player or to sign a star from another team who can help them for a season or two—even if that player is from a hated rival. Corporations have adopted a similar strategy and employees need to understand this, adapt to it, and even embrace it.

How can I look for new work while in my current job?

When you embrace this philosophy there are practical ways to look for your next job before you actually need it that don't have to compromise your current employer. Here are a few time-tested strategies:

Associate with "A" players. Surround yourself with the quality players in your current organization. Proverbs 13:20 is a powerful verse, *He who walks with the wise grows wise, but a companion of fools suffers harm.* This philosophy applies as much in our work as it does in any other part of our life. If you'll seek out the best performers and the best respected people in your organization, particularly those in roles similar to yours, you'll not only learn from them but you'll also begin to be associated with top performers. It's success by association (as opposed to guilt by association).

~ He who walks with the wise grows wise. Or, success by association! ~

I learned this lesson when I was first promoted into management at IBM. I was assigned as the manager in an office in Pasadena, California and had a team of 10 or so employees, most of whom were older and far more experienced than I was. I struggled a great deal in the first couple of months in that role. My Regional VP, "Ron," was astute enough to point out—more like shout out—my deficiencies. Nothing like a real shot in the arm to fire me up! After one particular meeting with Ron, I went home and told Devonie I was ready to quit because I didn't think I was cut out for this job, for IBM, or for being a manager.

The next day, having licked my wounds, I came to a career-changing conclusion: I was not associating with other successful people in this role. I had no one to mentor or teach me this new, challenging job. I decided to call the two most successful managers in that region, Monte Stern and Jack Lane, and I humbly admitted that I was really struggling. I shared that I could greatly benefit from their experience and advice. They both agreed to have me come spend time with them to see what was working and what wasn't. It was an ideal learning opportunity from two perspectives: 1) I learned from the best, and 2) I developed great relationships with two people who were likely to have success in the future

—including subsequent moves to new and higher level jobs either within IBM or elsewhere. I have now worked with Jack in four different companies, and he's still one of my dearest friends. Monte also went on to be highly successful both within IBM and as a senior executive with subsequent companies. Walk with the wise!

Be a diligent networker—always. This is one of the hardest things for most of us to do well, particularly when we're gainfully employed. It's difficult either because we get too busy to nurture our personal network of contacts or because we're introverted and uncomfortable with the whole process. The irony is that we often struggle to network because we're too busy working; yet when we really need to network (during a period of unemployment, for example), our "friends" are unresponsive because we've done a lousy job of staying in touch. This is the biggest regret I hear from people in job search.

The key to networking is to be consistent and diligent— not only for your personal benefit but also for the benefit of those you network with in the process. Here are some suggestions for nurturing your contacts:

- Be intentional and be efficient. Segment your contacts and business relationships into categories (A's B's and C's, or any categories that work for you) and keep in touch in different ways by category:
  - o A's— These are the friends and colleagues you most want to associate with and with whom you have the deepest relationship. This group is unlikely to exceed 10-20 people and you'll want to get together face-to-face at least once per year and touch base more frequently with no particular agenda or purpose.
  - o B's—This list may be +/- 50 people (a more extended set of friends) for most of us and

they are a group you'll always be on the lookout for how you can help/serve them either personally or professionally. Call them occasionally and e-mail more frequently (or send a hand-written card or note) to stay in touch and keep them abreast of where you are and what you're doing in work and beyond.

o C's—This group tends to be a broader set of social and work-related acquaintances that you'll periodically trade emails with or you'll pass along a helpful article- anything that adds value for them and keeps you and your association with them on their radar screen. Social networking sites like Facebook, My Space, and LinkedIn are great Internet-based tools that help you stay in touch (efficiently) with this larger set of people.

- Use the "netweaving" philosophy—an approach coined by Bob Littell in his book, *The Heart and Art of Netweaving: Building Meaningful Relationships One Connection at a Time*. Littell's premise is that networking is about giving to others first, and doing so in a genuine fashion by helping people you meet to connect with others you know – for the benefit of all. You'd be amazed how infrequently this approach is used by most people. The great thing about this strategy is that it can be used not only to distinguish yourself personally but more importantly to serve others and glorify God's light and spirit in you at the same time. I know countless examples of unemployed or mis-employed people who have been dejected when even personal friends haven't returned their call to help them network for their next opportunity. My challenge to you: all of us—particularly those of us who claim to have the love of Christ in us—have a responsibility to help those in need. And when someone is looking for work, it's a unique opportunity for us to serve them by "netweaving." Often, networking is a simple matter of introducing your friend Bill to your former neighbor George—for their mutual benefit. How hard can that be? These opportunities usually come at a time when that person may be most receptive to your sharing the message and promise of the gospel. Please don't miss this great opportunity!

- Volunteer - another great networking strategy is finding organizations or associations related to your field of interest and then offering your time to help at their annual industry meeting—perhaps calling to confirm participation or greeting guests as they arrive at an event, as examples. There are few better ways to meet people than helping on a project of this nature; and the people you meet may be in a position to help you in your next career transition, whenever that may occur.

Commit to lifelong learning. One of the most effective ways to look for your next role or job without really looking is to be a committed student long after your high school or college education days are over. Enroll in evening classes at a community college to learn more about business or accounting principles or even a foreign language. Maybe you register for a workshop through your company to enhance your presentation or listening skills. It might come in the form of web-based education/training modules or a specialized certification or degree for that matter. Regardless of the medium—keep learning because knowledge is value (and provides options). These learning opportunities also allow you to be exposed to new and different people in your fields of interest and you'll treasure these relationships in the future.

~ Knowledge = Value (and provides career options) ~

Define your career goals and objectives. How do you know if you're making progress in your career if you don't have well defined goals for your future? No company would operate without a strategic plan and a corresponding set of goals and objectives that underpin the strategy. Why shouldn't you do the same, particularly if you're convinced of the merits of the Me, Inc. philosophy? Do you know what job you'd like to have next? Do you know what role or function you want in five years? If you do, you're able to be far more intentional about how to get from where you are to where you intend to be. Those who make goal setting a priority are able to spend their "extracurricular" time in as productive a way possible, taking steps—even baby steps—toward these goals. Most importantly, establishing career goals will give you hope and enthusiasm for your future and keep you from being consumed by the day-to-day trials and tribulations of your current job without a hopeful eye to what lies ahead.

Be inquisitive about other people's work and careers. I may be unusual in this, but I thoroughly enjoy spending time with people to better understand their jobs:

- How did they get started in their line of work?
- What do they like best about their career? What's the worst part of the job?
- What advice do they have for others who might be interested in this career?

The more you know about how others have found fulfilling work, the better you'll be equipped to do the same. Get in the habit of being inquisitive and you'll be exposed to a variety of careers, some of which may also be a great fit for you. People love to talk about themselves; if you ask them to go to lunch so you can learn more about their job and seek their advice and counsel, they are more than likely to help.

Use the Internet. Countless resources on the Internet can help you to explore career options while you have a job (of course, don't do this while at work or on company time). A site like www.salary.com can help you stay abreast of your market value. Search agents such as www.indeed.com and www.simplyhired.com can do the hard work of scanning the web for career positions that are a good fit for your profile and will deliver the results to you as the best opportunities become available. This allows you to be proactive in scanning for career alternatives in relative privacy. And of course, for the less private alternatives - there's always the major job boards—www.monster.com, www.careerbuilder.com, www.sixfigurejobs.com, or www.linkedin.com, among a few hundred others, depending on your industry, job level, etc. Be as knowledgeable as possible about the vast resources literally at your fingertips. You don't even have to leave your desk to get most of this help.

Be willing to listen when you find new opportunities. Many workers are hesitant to explore new opportunities for fear that their employer will hear about it or because they don't want to be disloyal. In today's employment environment the prevailing worker philosophy must change. I've seen far too many employees victimized by unexpected dismissals and layoffs to think otherwise. The job market is a free market environment and it's most prudent for workers to explore alternative career opportunities—as long as you can do so without negatively impacting your current employer. There are at least three reasons why this philosophy is imperative for most workers:

- Even if the opportunity isn't a great fit, you'll learn from the experience. Some of what you learn may actually make you more effective in your current role.

- If the opportunity isn't a fit for you, you may know another candidate to refer to the potential employer — a great networking opportunity that benefits all.
- It may be a job that's too good to pass up!

Remember, this is no time to be apologetic about your desire to keep your personal career interests at the top of your mind and efforts. Be proactive in these efforts; the passive or complacent approach leaves far too many people flat-footed in their career progression or, worse yet, miserable in their current work. And, it's far easier to find a job when you have a job. Take advantage of this fact and make things happen!

What follows is a story that highlights the benefit of being proactive in seeking your next career opportunity – before you actually need it.

~ Preparing for the future today: Ash and Beth Merchant ~

Ash moved from upstate New York to the south as an 11-year-old and earned his business degree at the University of Georgia. His wife, Beth, earned her teaching degree at Berry College in Rome, Ga., and spent the first 11 years of her professional life in elementary education.

They married in 2001 and both worked full time until they celebrated the arrival of their son in 2004. "We decided from the start of our marriage that we would learn to survive on one income," Ash says. "Then when we started to have children, Beth would be able to be a stay-at-home mother."

Ash started his career with a worldwide staffing organization and was the proverbial corporate ladder climber—starting as a temp, advancing to sales roles, then branch manager, corporate staff positions, and ultimately district/market management over a 10-year period. "I was running the corporate race and doing well, but I wasn't particularly satisfied with the journey," he lamented.

Like many others in 2003, he fell victim to a layoff and admitted to being both arrogant and scared about his future prospects. "I finally realized when I became unemployed that I had done a poor job of developing and nurturing my personal and network relationships beyond the people I worked with directly," he recalls. "It's a lesson I'll never forget."

Ash jumped quickly at an offer to become the market manager in Georgia for a human resource benefits and outsourcing company. Beth had some reservations: "I didn't think it was a good move for Ash, and I told him so. But when he decided to take the position, I was committed to support him and not be the relentless dissenter."

During his time at this outsourcing company, Ash grew in his faith and began to see God as central to his life, his career, and his daily choices. Within 18 months he recognized that it was not the ideal work environment and once again started searching for the right fit.

"It was at this point that we became intentional in looking at career choices," Beth says. She and Ash sat down together and defined their key priorities. They agreed that minimum travel, little or no weekend and evening work for the sake of their son, and the flexibility to be involved in things like boy scouts and volunteering with the Crossroads Career Ministry were of highest importance. Aside from wanting Ash to earn enough for Beth to continue being a stay-at-home mom, compensation was low in their priorities.

As Ash was trying to determine where God wanted to plant him, he became an executive (half-time) with a start-up venture focused in the emerging field of consumer-directed healthcare. He also became a contract sales person for a recruiting firm in the Atlanta area. "I wasn't certain if I should run my own business, go to work for another large business, or be a contractor for multiple businesses," he says, "so I had a unique opportunity to test the market and my skills."

Ash is a prime example of finding a new job when you don't need one. He has also become a very successful networker. How? "Be persistent in sustaining key relationships; it's not enough to meet once and never connect again. Be genuine and transparent. People appreciate knowing your heart, and it's amazing how much they care when you build the right kind of trust and have a heart to help others. Networking is not about meeting people; it's primarily about helping others, and the rest takes care of itself."

During the 18 months of what he calls this career "experiment" stage, Ash found an opportunity with Aon Consulting, one of the largest HR consulting and risk management companies in the world. He has become a sales executive with Aon and has found his stride. In Beth's view, "he's successful, he comes home happy, and it's a job that is consistent with the priorities that we defined two years ago." They both view his individual contributor role as a gift from God.

"I used to be focused on my career ladder," Ash observes. "I've now come to believe that it's more about a career lattice—not focused on the next rung of the ladder, but open to lateral moves or even steps down for the optimum fit with my skills, interests, and priorities. I get to spend every day doing what I most enjoy, meeting new people and developing relationships."

Ash is also a testament to another lesson—the commitment to continuous learning. While with his first employer, he completed his MBA at Emory University (paid for by his employer). When he got involved in the start-up venture, he became licensed to sell insurance and financial products in support of their business. And in the last five years, he has become an expert on human resource related topics that are relevant to most corporations today because he has been a committed student of his profession. All of which makes him more valuable to a variety of potential employers both large and small.

Lessons Learned

Ash: "The workforce is filled with people who lack 'clarity' in life—which most often doesn't come from our work. I get comfort from Proverbs 3:5-6: *Trust in the Lord with all your heart and lean not your own understanding; in all your ways acknowledge Him, and He will make your paths straight.*"

Beth: "I cling to God's promise in Psalms 9:10: *Those who know your name will trust in you, for you, Lord, have never forsaken those who seek you.*"

Chapter 10 Reflection Questions:

- How does striving for excellence in your current work serve as an investment in your future career?
- What can you do to improve your opportunities to find the next great job with your current employer?
- Do you feel guilty about exploring new job opportunities while you're employed? Why or why not?
- Why is it easier to find a job when you have one?
- What can you do to explore new career opportunities with prospective employers? Is there any reason you wouldn't do that today, even passively?

Chapter 11:

Job Search Key Success Factors

—⚭—

There are plenty of books — 316,346 according to a recent search on Amazon.com — about the art and science of searching for a job. That topic is not my focus in either this chapter or this book. Instead, I want to share a few insights that can make a powerful difference in finding the right work for you – whether you are employed today or not.

I've had an opportunity over the past several years to personally witness (and coach) the job searches of several hundred people, and I've seen the good, the bad, and, in more cases than I would care to admit, even the ugly. I've also interviewed and hired hundreds of people over the course of my corporate career, and I've seen about every conceivable job search approach and scenario.

Just before I left Spherion in early 2003, I sensed a strong call to find a way to help those struggling with career transition. It felt as much from God as anything I had experienced previously; and when He calls, I'm learning to listen and to be obedient.

Devonie and I agreed that I would spend six months initially dedicated to finding out where God wanted me to spend my time and energy in alignment with His will and with the gifts and experiences he had blessed me with. I had a clear sense that my calling was related to the field of career transition because of my experience in the industry and the obvious fact that so many struggle immensely with employment challenges. In fact, it has become clear that career-related challenges represent a unique life "crisis" situation in which to introduce people to the promise of the gospel or, at a minimum, to help them strengthen their relationship with Christ in the process. As a friend of mine once said, "When we become unemployed, it's as though God knows that the only way we tend to look up towards heaven is when He knocks us on our back"

In typical Type "A" fashion, I proceeded to interview over 100 people who were either unemployed or mis-employed, or others who were career counselors and ministry leaders who help people with career transition challenges. I even interviewed the spouses of several career explorers to get their perspectives. I was focused on learning, helping where possible, and perhaps most importantly, determining where God wanted me to contribute. I wasn't sure if I was supposed to make my living in this arena or to be involved as an avocation and find another way to pay the bills. It became obvious, early in my exploration, that this was not the ideal way for me to try to make a living. It was equally obvious that there were great opportunities for me to help more than a few people and the journey allowed me to learn a great deal about what works and what's missing for people in the career search process today.

Based on this firsthand research and experience, my intent in this chapter is to highlight the few, most critical factors that seem to make the biggest difference for those who have been successful in finding work that's consistent with their God-given talents. If you'll combine these few "lessons learned" with the details you'll find in one or more of those 316,346 books available on Amazon (or check out the appendix of this book for a few highly recommended job search books), you'll likely fare well.

Don't walk alone

The job search process is a very lonely time for most people, particularly men. Most career explorers, as we call them in the Crossroads Career Ministry, feel as though they are very much alone in this process. In their previous job, they'd have a team of people working with them. They had regular meetings with their manager to report on progress and could ask for input and feedback on projects and activities. They always felt like they were part of a bigger organization where people would help each other, where they could develop personal and professional relationships, and even celebrate successes.

The job search journey, especially for the unemployed, is entirely different. Most people have very little interaction with anyone outside of their direct family unless it's an all-too-occasional phone call or cup of coffee with a friend. They feel pressure from all relationship sides—kids, spouse, and parents—although much of the pressure is self-imposed. They often admit to severe bouts of lost confidence and some are honest enough to admit they're depressed (although very few actually do anything about it). Except for some who may have the benefit of working with an outplacement firm, job seekers are largely left to fend for themselves. And the vast majority is not well-equipped to search for work effectively. The best strategy to employ may be to simply find some resources at the Department of Labor's unemployment office while they file for benefits.

All of this made it obvious to me that the most important priority for most in career transition is to stop walking the journey alone and start walking with others who share the same challenge.

Here's a parallel: many large churches have been creating a way to bring their congregation members into closer relationships by developing small group programs. In essence, they create a forum for six to eight adults or couples in a similar stage of life (age, location, children, etc.) to "do life" together in a Christ-centered way. They often meet weekly to build relationships, to help each other in a variety of circumstances, and to learn and study the Bible together.

This same small group approach is even more relevant and should be applied to those going through career transition. If a person struggling with unemployment or even those intent on searching for a better career alternative can find three to six other people who are willing to commit to walk the journey together and to stay together as a team until the entire small group of career explorer members find work, it will significantly enhance their effectiveness in the process. When initiated properly, it becomes an incredibly powerful forum for people to get practical, spiritual, and emotional support. It's an effective way to share lessons learned and great ideas and a means of holding each other accountable. It's also a forum to show others the love of Christ at a critical time in their life.

Here's a practical example: a person in career transition may know 50 people in their personal network that they can reach out to in the job search process. It doesn't take long to talk with each, and then what? Alternatively, if five men come together to form a small group and each of them knows 50 people in their personal network – and we resolve to proactively help each other in the journey, there are 5 times more personal contacts that may be able to help for each person in the group. This is a simple example of the practical advantage of the body of Christ coming together to help each other in times of need. As Ecclesiastes 4:12 says, *Though one may be overpowered, two can defend themselves. A cord of three strands* (us) *is not quickly broken.*

The concept is called Christ Centered Career Groups (go to www.C3G.org for free information on this approach and for suggestions on establishing your own group), and we have also integrated the philosophy as part of the broader Crossroads Career® Network (www.crossroadscareer.org) tools we make available to churches who want to start or enhance their own career ministry with this approach.

Grow your relationship with Jesus Christ

God has a purpose for everything. *We know that in all things, God works for the good of those who love Him and are called according to His purpose* (Romans 8:28). It's clear that God uses times of crisis to get our attention because He knows how difficult it is to get our attention when life is good. It's almost as though He grabs us by the collar and says, "I couldn't get your attention before this trial; I wonder if I can have it now." But for too many people who go through a job search, they never hear His call.

~ Sometimes we only look up (to God) when we get knocked on our back ~

There are few better opportunities for us to pause to examine our beliefs, our behaviors, and our relationship with God than during a job search, when we have more free time than most ever hope to have. Too often we compartmentalize God to Sundays and an occasional prayer before meals. Maybe this is *the* perfect time to wrestle with a few key questions:

- Do you know what His will is for your life and therefore for your career? Do you care?
- Do you know what God is teaching you in this time of trial and transition?

- Is this an opportunity for you to spend quiet time with your Creator every morning to pray, learn, and discern His will for you?

God is zealous to have a relationship with you. And He's willing to do whatever it takes to reach you, including giving you some extra time (and challenges) to ponder all of this. If you end up finding your next job without growing closer to Him in the process, you've missed a huge opportunity. The most important relationship in your life and in your eternal future is your relationship with Jesus. Discover what God is trying to teach you. Is it to spend more time with Him? To be a better steward of financial resources? To learn humility? To grow closer to your wife and/or your children? Job search is, for many, among the best opportunities to be still and to grow closer to God in the journey because our dependence should be on Him, not our work.

Be clear about your interest and direction

One of the common mistakes career explorers make is trying to cast their search net as wide as possible to try to catch any kind of fish in the sea of opportunities. Like one candidate said, "I've had experience in accounting functions like accounts payable, purchasing, and payroll processing. I've also been in customer service and really enjoy it. And I've even had experience in sales because I worked in a call center where we were challenged to up-sell and cross-sell other products. So I'm really qualified to do a number of things—do you have any opportunities that fit these experiences?"

What do you think the person on the other end of this discussion heard in all of that? In essence, you're a jack of all trades and a master of none. It's not very clear what you're really good at doing. And, it's also not obvious what you're most *interested* in doing.

A large portion of career explorers are guilty of this wide net approach. What an employer would really like to hear—and what tends to differentiate one candidate from 50 (or 500) others competing for the same role may sound more like, "I've had a diversity of experience in accounting and customer service related areas but I have discovered that I am ideally suited for and most successful in a direct selling role where I have the opportunity to open new account relationships and expand those relationships over time."

What's different about this answer? It's clear that you have a good, diverse background. And yet, you're sure of what you want in your next job and you're confident and self-aware enough to state it succinctly. The potential employer who hears the second answer is far more likely to proceed to the next step in the process because employers want prospective employees who know what they're good at doing and are clear about where they want to be.

You may be thinking, "But I don't want to pigeonhole myself into one area. What if there are great opportunities in a number of different roles?" It's okay to have two or three potential careers you'd be satisfied with. But you can't afford to say them all to any given employer or network contact. For example, it's fine to use the second script above for a potential employer who wants to fill a sales opening, but if you're interested in an accounts payable position for a particular company, you need to convince this employer that accounts payable is *the* job you're most interested and qualified to do. Make it obvious that you're very clear on what you want and ensure your resume(s) communicate this well!

Identify and <u>proactively</u> pursue target companies

Think of this in marketing terms. When a company wants to take a new product to the market, it's very specific about its target markets: the age of potential buyers, their gender, ethnicity, geographic areas, income strata, etc.

Why wouldn't a career explorer take the same approach? By defining the target companies that would be a good fit for your skills, experience, and interests, you're far better equipped to proactively find a position in these companies. Simply waiting until you hear about an opportunity and then trying to compete by submitting your resume via the career tab on the company's web site is about like spending a dollar on the lottery – it may payoff but likely won't.

I'll commonly ask career explorers about their career goals and targets. The all-too-common response sounds something like, "I'd like to take my experience in information technology to a large company in the Atlanta area." What's missing from this answer?

The listener gleans the following: "You know what function you're targeting but little else. It sounds like you haven't done much homework on good companies to work for that also fit your skills. And I don't really know how I can help you much." You'll most likely get nothing but a polite, "nice to meet you and good luck in your job search." Perhaps they'll patronizingly even say, "I'll keep my eyes out for you."

Here's what it sounds like when you're clear on your target companies: "Because of my experience in the retail industry and my knowledge of the IBM mid-range systems, I am excited about the prospect of working for Home Depot or The Federated Group here in Atlanta."

~ Identify target companies and then go <u>find</u> a job, don't wait for one to show up ~

What's different this time? The person on the other end of this conversation is very clear that the career explorer knows where they want to work, who they want to work for, and why they want to work there. In addition—and I'm not sure I can fully explain this phenomenon—I've found that people's ability to help you in your career search is highly dependent on their knowledge of specific companies you mention in the conversation. Try it both ways; you'll see that people are many times more likely to suggest a helpful network contact—maybe their neighbor works for Home Depot or their former manager now works at Federated—simply because you mentioned these companies. Clarity matters.

The steps to establish your best company targets are pretty simple, but they may take some research and time. Once you've clearly defined the direction you're pursuing and the criteria for the industry, role, culture, etc., you're aiming for, then take the time to find 10-20 companies that are a good fit for you. Armed with this list, the job search then becomes a proactive approach to gaining access, finding referrals, and doing research to discover if and where the opportunities exist within these companies. In contrast, the career explorer who doesn't use a target company list and employs an opportunistic approach to the entire spectrum of potential organizations spends his or her time waiting to hear about opportunities or trolling the Internet to see what might appear. They'll see job openings coming available with random companies and those companies may not even be a good fit. I'd rather bet on the success of the person with the proactive approach. I'd also predict a much higher level of satisfaction with the job they land.

There's one more advantage to this approach. Notice the reaction when a potential employer hears a job search candidate say, "I've done my homework and research, and I understand my own skills well enough to know that I'm intent on working for your organization." They'll look surprised and impressed because so few people are this clear and have this level of conviction about their goals. Clarity and conviction are exactly what most employers are looking for. Use them to your advantage!

Networking, networking, networking

In Chapter 10, we identified the importance of being an effective networker while you're still employed. When you're in active job search mode, networking becomes all the more critical.

I know I won't shock any readers with this flash of brilliance, but it's worth stating nonetheless: You aren't likely — although it does happen occasionally — to find your next career opportunity via the Internet. Online sources are good for researching career possibilities, but they aren't great job leads. Over 80 percent of open positions are filled through word of mouth, friend of a friend, or any other referral based on relationships. That fact makes it easy to convince career explorers that networking is a must. Unfortunately, that doesn't make it any easier or less intimidating for the average person, particularly those who are more introverted.

If you're intimidated by the notion of networking, here are some simple ways to overcome your trepidation:

- Start with friends and people who know you and your skills, including those from your past. Don't just think about networking with those you've known or worked with most recently. What about the previous six companies you've worked for over the past 15-20 years? They aren't that hard to find if you make the effort, thanks to the Internet. When you connect with these old friends and colleagues, ask them who else they have stayed in touch with over the years – this is partially a numbers game. There are also useful websites that can be helpful in finding former contacts: www.whitepages.com, www.classmates.com, www.zoominfo.com, www.linkedin.com.
- Give first. This is counter-intuitive for the average, stressed-out job seeker who's most interested in getting help, not giving it. Just try a change in your

orientation. Find ways to help those you meet with. Can you connect them with someone you know who could be helpful to them? How can you give them knowledge about something you've learned — perhaps a useful career-related meeting or a resource you found on the Internet? You'll find that when you start with this mindset, you begin to build the roots of trust that are so critical and useful to the whole networking process. And it happens to be consistent with God's second greatest commandment: love others as yourself (Matthey 22:39). What a great concept, huh?

- Be realistic about your objectives in a networking/ referral type of meeting. Don't approach these meetings with the goal of finding a job. Expect only to get to know the other person better and perhaps receive some good counsel for your search. People seem far more willing to give advice than to find you a job. Most networking meetings are successful if they result in one or two additional referrals that can help you expand your contacts, give you more insight, and perhaps point you to some opportunities in your sweet spot.

- Swallow your pride. Many people looking for a job tend to be afraid, maybe even ashamed to admit being out of work. This is obviously counterproductive in job search. The most effective job seekers are those who aren't ashamed and who follow the "three foot rule." Anybody within three feet of you (at church, at the movie theater, at your child's soccer game, etc.) ought to know you're in career transition. Without knowing, they can't help you! You never know when and how God is going to put someone in your path that will be helpful in this process. In fact, the most effective job seekers are borderline "proud" to share their career transition with anyone they come in contact with. They effectively explain why they're enthusiastic about what the future holds. "This search is giving me a great opportunity to explore some new personal and professional directions," they'll say, turning what many perceive as a negative situation into a positive. With this approach, you'll be delighted by how many people respond to your positive attitude with a willingness to help you in a variety of ways, perhaps even opening the door to some of their key contacts.

• Get your spouse on your team. One common challenge many job searchers struggle with is their relationship with their spouse. Your spouse can be one of the best networkers on your team. But small cracks in a marriage often turn into a chasm when one of you has to look for a job. The unemployed spouse may feel pressure, while the other feels fear. The antidote is to invest some time in each other to draw closer and become a team in this process. If you're like me, even small struggles in your marriage can negatively impact your effectiveness in your other roles and responsibilities. You can't afford to let that seep into your interviewing, networking, or other relationships. Take this time in career transition to invest in your marriage. Make time for your spouse that you didn't have when you were working. This can be one of the biggest blessings of the whole career transition; it certainly was for my marriage. Another side benefit for men is that our wives tend to know more people and have deeper relationships with more people than we do. When they become an integral part of the process, including networking, great things can happen. You and your spouse are a team, so act like it and enjoy the fruits that will last far beyond the career search.

Crossroads Career® Explorer Guide

The Crossroads Career® Network, and specifically its founder Brian Ray, have developed an outstanding curriculum that can help you walk through your career transition. It's available for free to anyone who has purchased this book! This curriculum is a Christ-centered resource that includes a six-step process for anyone struggling with career options — whether employed and unhappy or unemployed and seeking new work. It helps you through the journey with scripture verses, exercises, thought-provoking tips, and opportunities for reflection. This resource can be used either individually or, better yet, more collaboratively in a small group of career explorers. Just click on the "Register Here" link on the Crossroads Career Network website at www.crossroadscareer.org and use the promotion code "betterway" for a free, one year subscription to these resources for Career Explorers (a $40 value).

Final thought

When you find yourself in job search mode, don't just try to work at it harder than anyone else; work smarter than anyone else. And don't walk this journey alone. Keep God at the center of your search (and your life) and accept the fact that He's in control and you aren't! Your next job opportunity may not come in your ideal timing, but it will come in God's divine and blessed timing.

Chapter 11 Reflection Questions:

- What have you found to be the most challenging elements of a formal job search?
  - o   Interviewing?
  - o   Networking?
  - o   Using the Internet?
  - o   Other?
- If you're in an active search, how can you find others in the same journey and create a Christ Centered Career Group for accountability, encouragement, and networking support?
- When you're networking, is your focus on getting help or giving help? How can you lend more help to others?
- What resources are available to help you make career search process? (I invite you to go to the Crossroads Career® Network website www.crossroadscareer. org and use the promotion code "betterway" for free access to the Career Explorer Guide—a step-by-step process to walk through your career transition in a Christ-centered way—and a host of additional resources, articles, and other helpful links.)

Chapter 12

Worker Generations: Young, Mid-Career, and the 50+ Crowd

—ᴍ—

As the world of work continues to evolve, the implications for all workers are profound; but, they're different in subtle and sometimes significant ways for each generation. There isn't a one-size-fits-all formula for flourishing. Those raised in the baby-boom generation, for example, have a different set of challenges, are driven by a different set of motivations, and make decisions based on very different criteria than Gen-Y and Gen-X workers. Let's explore some of the major implications of these workplace differences for four major categories of workers.

Young Millennials: high school and college students

The changing set of work rules, a struggling public education system, even an emerging set of new careers can seem a bit daunting to the average young person. Perhaps some simple recommendations will help you thrive in your future career:

Be a student forever. When you graduate with your diploma, your days of learning are not over. You'd be wise to make a lifelong commitment to experiencing new things, learning new skills, and staying abreast of changing technologies and trends in order to achieve your personal and professional goals. Sometimes the learning comes in the form of extra-curricular activities or hobbies you may develop.

Here's a simple example: how much more valuable is the worker today who understands how to develop and leverage a website on the Internet? Very! You can use this skill to find new work or promote a new business idea. You can even use it to help support a church or ministry you have a heart to support. You're even likely to find employment opportunities for experienced web developers in multiple industries, all the more reason to keep learning and developing these and other new skills and put them to use in areas that most interest you. As our economy continues to evolve to a knowledge based economy (versus Industrial for much of the 1900's), the most valuable "core" skills for young workers to master for the foreseeable future:

- Personal organizational skills – plan your work and work your plan
- Communications skills – beneficial for every trade and career
- Logic and reasoning skills – math and science skills are still in vogue
- Internet and technology – The engine that's driving today's economy
- Specialized vocational skills – from auto mechanic to medical technicians and beyond

Don't be consumed or overwhelmed if you don't yet have a clear view of the perfect job or career. Very few actually have that clarity before they get into the work world for a few years, and some never find it. Based on your interests and passions (see Chapter 5), find work that's at least a reasonable fit for you and go for it. You can't be paralyzed by an obsession to find the single best fit because there are likely hundreds of jobs you could enjoy and perform well. The more experience you have with each job—and you are likely to have more than 13 employers in the course of your career—the better clarity you will gain on what you like and don't like.

My oldest daughter Kelly is an example of this; she graduated in 2005 with a degree in speech communications and a minor in English from the University of Georgia. Upon graduation she declared, "I don't have any idea what I want to do!" And she was terribly intimidated because life tells us that we must know by age 22 what the rest of our life will look like—which just isn't realistic. Kelly decided to try teaching high school English and spent 15 months getting her master's degree in secondary English education. She's discovered that she is gifted in her ability to teach and reach high school kids and likes making a difference in their lives. Even if she chooses another path down the road, she's had a great experience and is all the more valuable to future employers. Sometimes you won't know if you'll like something until you try it—and if you don't like it, try something else. In the grand scheme of life, it's okay.

Young workers (22-29 years old)

This is an intimidating time of life for most young workers because there's so much that's unknown. What lies ahead? Will I be successful? What if I'm not? What if I choose the wrong path? All are common questions for workers in their 20s. Here's some lessons learned for this group to help you flourish in the new world of work:

Explore and experiment. The goal at this stage of your career is to gain a diversity of experience—either within one company or even with a few. This enables you to get a first-hand perspective on what you like, what you don't like, and what you're good at doing. In essence, you're trying to determine your God-given gifts and talents in order to leverage them in the balance of your career. I've seen young workers who start in a career that is neither fun nor fulfilling and yet they stay in this line of work for 10 or more years simply because they were too complacent to experiment with other paths. The easiest time to experiment is early in your career – before you have the obligations (and bills) that you'll likely add in your 30's and beyond.

Keep financial commitments manageable. Few things limit a working person's career flexibility more than having heavy debts and expenses. They can quickly force us to stay with the job we have, regardless of how little we enjoy the work. Workers who are careful not to spend all they earn— and save effectively—are able to make career adjustments in order to pursue the work that God has made them for. Doing so requires that you learn the value of being content with less (money) and in exchange, you're more likely to have a career that satisfies versus one that simply pays the bills. In this case, less really is more.

Keep learning, The same principle I mentioned above for students still applies. Just because you finished high school or college doesn't mean your learning days are over. Commit yourself to a lifetime of learning—adapting your skills in your chosen career to the new technologies and dynamics in the market. When we get "stale," we quickly become less competitive in the job market.

Take responsibility for your own savings, retirement, and health insurance. The time to get this right is when you're in your 20s. You can't rely on any one corporation (or the government) to provide your pension or your long-term healthcare. Participate fully in your 401k or deferred compensation programs and seriously consider starting your own health savings account (HSA), either in cooperation with your employer or independently. You'll be amazed at how much you're able to accumulate for your future needs—and it will accumulate in *your* hands, beyond the reach of legislative whims.

Seek career mentors. Create an "inner circle" of sorts that you can call on to provide advice and counsel as you consider career alternatives and wrestle with difficult issues related to work. Proverbs 13:20 says it well, *He who walks with the wise grows wise, but the companion of fools suffers harm.* Tap into the experience and wisdom of those that have walked ahead of you in life and in their careers.

Keep work in its proper perspective. The early stage of your career is where your perspectives are developed and your habits are ingrained. The more you understand where work fits into your life now, the less vulnerable you'll be to allow work to consume your time, energy, and ego later in life when you have a marriage, children, and other critical priorities. Workaholics in today's world of work are usually "birthed" in the first 8-10 years of your career when tendencies become habits and habits become tough to break. Remember to stay "centered" on Christ to maintain your work-life balance.

Gen X: mid-career workers

Workers between 30 and 50 years old usually have a different set of individual, family, and career dynamics than their younger counterparts. Most have had diverse enough experience to have a good sense of their skills and interests and have determined their specialized skills/roles that organizations value. Following are some practical career suggestions for this group:

Become a subject matter expert (SME). One important way to create distinction that also provides value to any number of employers is to become a SME in your chosen specialty area. Examples include a human resource professional who becomes an expert in labor relations (managing unions) or in acquiring technology-competent talent from other countries, or an accountant that specializes in internal auditing. Every employee who can create unique differentiation and depth of knowledge in a specific, highly relevant subject will fare better than a "generalist" in finding work or progressing in a career.

Keep learning. Sound familiar? The more you know the more valuable you become and the more competitive you will be in the employment market. Invest your time and energy in staying abreast of new skills, new technologies, and new strategies in your functional area of expertise. This becomes more challenging as we get older!

It's never too late to change careers. Too many workers get to this stage of their career and conclude that they are destined to continue on the same career path they've pursued in the past. One more time: God does not sentence us to a lifelong journey in work that doesn't fit our skills and interests. Be bold and brave enough to evaluate your priorities, make the necessary adjustments for a career change, and trust that God will honor your obedience to His calling. It sure beats living a life of quiet desperation.

Reduce your dependency on any one employer. Much of this book has been focused on helping every reader recognize that the loyalty and long-term employment environment of the '60s and '70s or even the 80's no longer exists. That doesn't mean it's impossible to have a 30 year career with one company; it still happens, probably more so in government jobs than anywhere else. But it's still important to manage your career by consistently evaluating your options and proactively exploring opportunities in the market. This will mitigate your risk of being surprised by an unexpected layoff and will likely enhance your long-term value and ultimately your success.

Evaluate non-traditional employment models. This career stage is perfect for finding alternative ways to provide your skills to companies on a contract or part-time basis.

Refer to chapter 8 for more on the paradigm shift to the Me, Inc. mentality.

Plan for your own financial and health future. The message is the same one we outlined with the 20 something workers above, but doubly important at this stage because there's less time available to save and plan effectively for your future.

What about the 50-plus crowd?

Although it may seem like a world away for some readers, there does come a time when you hit the big "five-OH!" At this stage, if you've had children, they're either approaching or beginning college or are living as independent, productive adults who are off your "payroll." Your costs begin to go down for the first time in more than 25 years—fewer cars to insure, less food to buy, maybe even a smaller house.

Many in this stage of life begin to feel restless. They may look back on the first 30 or so years of their career and decide that it's time to make a change. Maybe they've grown dissatisfied with their career choice and feel that it's the ideal time to look at better options. Some now have the practical and financial flexibility to explore career alternatives. And some may suddenly find themselves replaced by a younger (and less expensive) person in their current company.

The good news is that the employment demographics and the probable trajectory of our economy are likely to provide a positive employment environment for at least two decades, even (or perhaps especially) for older workers. There are projected to be plenty of available jobs, a shortage of available workers, and a great opportunity for those who choose (or need) to work into their 60s and 70s.

Regardless of your circumstance, you'll eventually face the challenge of determining what work you'd like to do in your 50s and beyond. The questions this age group struggles with include: What would I like to spend my time doing in the "second half" of my adult life? How long will I need to work? Do employers view me differently than they do younger workers—and is their perception advantageous for me or not? And for some, how can I finish my life and career well? Let's look at some of the practical lessons for this seasoned group:

Don't kid yourself—employers view you differently. Like it or not, employers look at the 50-plus workers differently than they do others. There are positive and negative aspects to this. On one hand, most employers recognize that a "senior" worker has far more experience than their younger counterparts and is therefore likely to be more effective and productive in a shorter period of time. On the other hand, they worry about several potential risks associated with older workers:

- Will they have the health and energy to be productive?
- Will they be motivated to work as hard as someone younger?
- Are they likely to retire soon, leaving the company with an unplanned opening?
- Do they even *need* to work, or does this job serve mostly to keep them occupied?
- Can they learn as quickly as their younger counterparts in today's tech world?
- Is our company more vulnerable to charges of age discrimination by hiring older workers and then, if they turn out not to be a good fit, deciding later to let them go?

The often hard-to-face reality is that employers worry about these issues. No, they'll never come out and ask the questions above, but they'll definitely consider them and may opt for younger workers as a result. It's important to recognize these realities and employ strategies and tactics to deal with them proactively.

Take advantage of your age. It's easy to feel victimized when you reach your mid-50s because you get the sense that you're not competing as effectively as you once did. Don't! The "victim" attitude serves no useful purpose to you or potential employers. Instead, turn this potential disadvantage into an advantage.

Be open to a variety of employment models. The more flexible you are to consider options—part-time, contract, project-based, or perhaps even job-sharing—the better your alternatives are likely to be. These types of options serve several useful purposes for the employer. They can mitigate the risk of hiring someone full time; they allow the employer to "try before they buy;" and they provide the company with maximum flexibility when business conditions change. Remember, they always have the option of converting a great part-time employee to full-time status if you prove your talents and their business conditions warrant. You've invested about 30 years of your life in a profession that has now made you an expert in certain functions. Why not parlay this expertise into your second-half career strategy. You can be a consultant for one or more of your previous employers—and you'll be productive immediately because you understand the company environment. Or, take your expertise to new employers.

When you're able to retire, don't! (But work on your terms) It may be that you're approaching the long-sought-after retirement stage and are now trying to figure out what to do with the rest of your life. You may have enough saved and not need to work, or maybe your plan is to supplement your retirement savings with part-time work. For others, there's no visible light at the end of the tunnel because there's not enough savings to support your retirement needs and the long term health of the Social Security system is highly suspect.

~ If a man will not work, he shall not eat ~

Whatever your circumstances, think carefully about the prudence of retirement—and specifically about what the Bible has to say on the topic. It actually encourages the opposite, *If a man will not work, he shall not eat* (2 Thessalonians 3:10). It's pretty clear: work in some form is God ordained for all of us. And there are lots of reasons to work in our 50's and beyond:

- We need the money—either today or in planning for our future. Healthcare costs alone can cause us to worry about our future financial needs.
- Work allows us to be generous and to make "eternal" investments.
- We need the challenge. Without challenges, we tend to get complacent. And when we stop learning, it leads to mental and physical atrophy.
- We need the affirmation. Human beings need to know we're making a contribution to a project, a business, or another person. Without this sense of contribution, our sense of worth suffers—and with it goes our outlook on life.
- Work gives us confidence and boredom breeds discontent.

This stage of life represents a great opportunity for workers to seek work that suits them, particularly if you have the opportunity to "right size" your expenses as your children are grown and some of the major expense obligations begin to fade into history. For the first time in your life you may be able to consider career options with more modest pay that ideally fit your skills, interests, and experience.

Stay young—mentally and physically. To compete in any marketplace, you have to have the skills, energy, knowledge, and stamina to be successful. As anyone who has been in competitive sports knows, the only way to do so is to exercise your mental and physical muscles.

The same applies to our aging minds and bodies. If we let them atrophy, we lose. Science has proven that exercising both mind and body keeps them working and equips you to live a longer, more satisfying life. Here are a few challenging questions to ponder:

- How often do you exercise? (It only requires 30 minutes a day, four days a week to stay reasonably fit.)
- What's the last new skill or activity you learned? A sport? A hobby? A class?
- Do you make the time to exercise your mind with puzzles? Intriguing books? New computer programs?

The more mentally and physically fit you are, the more competent you'll appear to others.

Mentor others—and share your hard-earned wisdom. A good friend of mine who recently turned 50 lamented in a small group discussion, "I only recently figured out that I was old enough and experienced enough to share my insights and lessons learned with others. I've always thought of myself as too young and inexperienced to make much of a contribution." He just had to give himself permission to share his wisdom. What investments are you making in others that allow them to gain the benefit of your seasoned insights and experiences?

~ Invest your *experience* in a younger worker ~

Bob Buford wrote a book a few years ago called, *Halftime: Changing Your Game Plan from Success to Significance*. He explains that we tend to spend the first half of our career trying to accumulate—money, knowledge, experience, etc. After this metaphorical halftime stage, we tend to shift to "contributing." The parallel is the shift from "success" to "significance." We'd all be wise to figure out how to best make the transition. That doesn't mean you have to stop working to achieve significance. It does mean, though, that you'll benefit from finding ways to feel this sense of contribution and significance.

One more for all workers:
Save and plan for retirement, but don't obsess about it. Every worker needs to plan for retirement or semi-retirement in some form. But there's a fine line between effectively planning for retirement and being obsessive about it. Clearly it's in your best interest to be a diligent saver and planner to create a secure "second half" of your adult life. It's also easy to be lulled into a sense of complacency or to procrastinate, intending to save more later in life. The stark reality is that if you don't start early, your chances of having even a modest retirement nest egg are slim.

Try to take full advantage of your company's 401k savings plan that allows your pre-tax contributions (and, in many cases, a company matching contribution) to grow over the course of your career. It may seem difficult to maximize this contribution, but the sooner you learn to live without that automatic deduction, the sooner you'll feel secure about your financial future. For workers over 50, there's even a "catch up" clause in our tax laws that allows you to accelerate your contributions in your later work years.

Final thoughts

There are unique challenges for every generation of workers today, but they're certainly not insurmountable. With a dose of preparation and a fair degree of diligence, there's a great opportunity for all of us to find a better way to make a living...and a life.

Chapter 12 Discussion Questions:

- What are you doing to prepare for your future that is unique to your career stage?
- What do you see as the biggest threats to your career at this stage?
- How effectively and proactively have you planned for your "second half" career? How specific are your plans? How flexible are they?
- Where does God fit in your journey as you plan for your future? Are you open to redirection and sensitive to the ways He may guide you?

Section IV

The Journey: Stand at the Crossroads and Look...

—ɯ—

This is what the LORD says: "Stand at the cross-roads and look; ask for the ancient paths, ask where the good way is, and walk in it, and you will find rest for your souls." —Jeremiah 6:16

I hope by now you're convinced that there's a better way to make a living...and a life. It may even be in your current job and career. If it's not, and if you're serious about making the journey to your intended destination—the remainder of this book is for you.

Your journey will require planning, diligence, and persistence to achieve your objectives. You'll find that it will be intimidating, especially during times of trial and challenge. For most, it promises to be exhilarating. When you decide to make changes in your career and in your life, you create a hope for your future that complacent workers rarely, if ever, experience.

We'll start by defining the components to develop a plan for your journey (Chapter 13) and then explore the common impediments and the keys to persisting (Chapter 14). In the final chapter (15), we'll unpack what it really means to experience God's peace in your work and in your life.

You'll find a template on our website (www.betterway-tomakealiving.com) that will assist you in developing your own personal inventory related to key concepts in the book as you seek clarity on your purpose, your calling, and your priorities and then develop a plan to help you achieve your goals. I pray that this journey will lead you to the fulfilling life God intended for you to experience — full of the love and peace He promises His faithful "workers."

Chapter 13

Plan: To Achieve Your Goals

—ↄↄↄ—

As you've wrestled with your purpose, calling, priorities, and God's perspective on your work, you've likely come to one of two conclusions. (1) Perhaps you've decided that you're in the right line of work—the role God has designed you for and for you. You may or may not be with the right employer or in the right employment model (employee versus contractor, for example), but you've determined that you're in the right field. Maybe you've even decided that the change most needed is not the work but your attitude about your work—a new, Christ-centered perspective on your purpose and priorities in work and life. (2) You've concluded you need a change in your work in order to better leverage your God-given gifts and talents. If so, hopefully you have (or will) identify two or three potential career alternatives that represent a better way for you. In either case, this chapter will help you reach your intended goals.

Remember, you're approaching the hardest part of this journey. The easiest, most common path taken by most is to do nothing at all. Doing nothing, of course, doesn't mean someone is happy in their current work environment; they just assume that changing careers is more work than it's worth. And yet, for most of us work is the biggest time commitment we make in our lives and it's worth the effort to find the right kind.

Much of what's covered in this chapter is related to getting your costs and finances in alignment with your career goals. The reason is simple: too many workers aren't able to pursue their calling and career aspirations because they don't have the financial flexibility to do so. I'm hopeful that we can identify some ideas to help you pursue your desire.

For those brave and faithful enough to walk this journey to a better way, here are some important steps to consider:

Create your vision

I'm a believer in the power of visualization. If you can visualize the outcome you desire, the odds are better that you, with God's provision, can achieve the outcome. I'll confess that when I play golf I'm not the best example of this concept. When I stand on a tee box preparing to hit my 6-iron 160 yards over a pond, my mind tends to be filled with negative thoughts, "Watch out for the water. Don't hit it fat. Don't hit it thin..." The prudent golfer does the opposite. He or she visualizes a perfect trajectory, easily clearing the water and landing softly on the green 25 feet from the pin. Perhaps this explains why I struggle to break a score of 90 after 40 years of playing golf.

There's a lesson here for developing a career plan. Start with defining and documenting a vision for where you're aiming. Define your goal in this process by describing your desired destination and try to be as specific as you can be at this point in the process. It may be somewhat vague at the start of the journey, but it will come into better focus as you make progress. One way to define the vision is to complete the following sentence, "I'll know I'm successful in this endeavor when_____." Here's an example:

"I'll know I'm successful in this endeavor when I've transitioned to become a medical technician by the end of 2009, having completed all of the necessary training and certification, and I'm employed by a medical office or hospital in the greater Houston area; earning a salary of at least $34,000. I'm excited about the prospect of doing this work that I feel uniquely gifted for, and I'll be working a more reasonable number of hours and with less stress than I currently experience in my work."

The vision doesn't have to be too complicated, but it does need to be well thought out and an accurate description of the end goal. If you're considering more than one potential career path, create a similar vision statement for each. This alone may help you refine your thinking about which option is most attractive and fits your priorities. The simple act of documenting your vision and goal will be a major step forward in this journey. Without one, you're likely to lack the enthusiasm and excitement that becomes the fuel for this journey.

Spouse alignment – better together

If you're married, it's important to ensure that you're well aligned with your spouse. A marriage is a partnership and with this partnership comes responsibility and opportunity. I've witnessed too many situations where a person decided to head down a new career path without thoroughly considering and consulting their spouse, only to find out a year or two later that part of their struggle (and perhaps lack of success) is due to their spouse not buying into the plan. If you can't work together toward the same goal, the odds of success become much lower. That's why chapter 6 discussed the importance of identifying not only your priorities but also those of your family.

The "checks and balances" of a marriage are not just an obstacle to overcome. They can also be a very beneficial asset. A spouse's vision can, if it aligns with yours, confirm the direction God is leading you; or, if it doesn't align with yours, serve as an important red flag to let you know to continue seeking God's will.

In a way, married couples in the workplace have an advantage over singles when it comes to creating career alternatives and aligning them with priorities. You have more options:

- Both spouses work full time
- Both spouses work part time
- One spouse works, the other stays home to raise the children
- One spouse works full time, the other part time

Even the nature of the work that the couple chooses to pursue can be highly complementary (only one spouse travels, the other is never, or rarely out of town for example). There are plenty of work options for married couples to consider, and it's likely that every possible option has been tried and made to work. The key for most couples is open communication, collaboration, and compromise to get to the right answer for your marriage and family. Take advantage of the gift of this asset called marriage and know that two people are better than one. That's how God designed marriage in the first place.

> ~ *"Too many people spend money they haven't earned to buy things they don't need to impress people they don't like."*
> **Will Rogers** ~

Assess and reduce your costs

Excessive expenses seem to be the biggest impediment to finding a better way to make a living...and a life. The obvious reason: once your costs and obligations rise to a certain level, your career options are reduced. There are fewer careers that pay $100,000 per year than those that pay $60,000 per year; and fewer at $60,000 than there are at $40,000; and so on. You may wonder if a family of four can live on $50,000 a year. The answer is yes. Will they drive new cars every four years? No. Will they vacation at Disney World? No. Will they live in Southern California? Probably not. But if this family is wise about their expenses, they're likely to have more time for each other, more family meals together, and a better appreciation for life's simple pleasures.

In fact, author Jean Chatzky argues in her book *You Don't Have to Be Rich* that money's ability to make us happy is very limited. Her study of 1,500 Americans suggests that happiness plateaus at a household income of $50,000.[29] This means that once you pass this income level, you won't experience any greater satisfaction—and you'll probably have more headaches, less free time, and more obligations.

I've been down this path and can tell you firsthand that the cycle is endless. In fact, when I was 35 years old I adopted a personal philosophy that I never wanted to earn an income that I couldn't easily replace with another company in a reasonable period of time. Otherwise, I'd feel entirely trapped by my current employer. That's the reason I left Andersen Consulting when I did. They offered to nominate me for "Partner" with an income three times more than I had ever made. It actually scared me—a lot. Especially combined with my workaholic tendencies, I felt as though this would put handcuffs on me that I couldn't remove. I started my job search almost immediately after I heard the news and left the firm within six months.

Here's another "lesson learned:" whatever income you earn, you'll find a way to spend it. Many of us get caught in this trap, and it's hard to break the cycle. As my salary increased over my career, we first bought a boat, then a vacation house, and some nice vacations . . . you know the pattern. These things *did* allow us to have some fun times as a family. But I'm not convinced they added any fulfillment or peace to our lives. They did, however, create some stress— more bills to pay and more things to maintain. And none of these "things" brought me closer to God. To the contrary, they pulled me further away because of the distractions they tended to create. Once again, it's all about the priorities and the trade-offs— and living a more purpose-driven life.

~ When your income increases, don't change your spending for one year ~

The U.S. is a consumer-driven culture, and this consumerism is the fuel that pushes many to the brink of bankruptcy—or worse yet, a coronary. We always want more: bigger homes, more expensive cars, and more high-tech gadgets. You name it, we want it. The sub-prime and related banking "credit" crisis of recent years highlights the nature of our culture today – and too many families spending beyond their means ultimately leads to financial disaster for families and eventually businesses. This all-too-recent crisis almost took Wall Street down with it. I can picture God watching us in disgust and musing, "They're reaping exactly what they sowed."

One of the big implications of our lack of spending discipline is that it limits our career flexibility. High spending often removes our option of making less money; of having one spouse stay at home with the kids; of choosing a more fulfilling career; of working part time; or of doing more charitable or ministry-related work. The bigger our bills, the less flexibility we have.

Here are the typical laments of those I've visited with who are caught in the trap of their own financial obligations:

- "I can't afford to make less than I make now, so I certainly can't change careers."
- "We're used to a certain lifestyle and my family wouldn't understand."
- "All of our neighbors are able to take great vacations. We should be able to do so as well."
- "I can't seem to jump off the treadmill. The more we earn, the more we spend. The more we spend, the less time we have to enjoy what we've spent."

Sound familiar? If so, I say: stop the insanity!

There is hope, but it requires hard, counter-cultural choices. Here are some of the keys to success gleaned from everyday people who have broken the "spending and debt" spiral:

- *Tithe.* One of the best ways to break the hold money has on us is to give it away—not frivolously, but responsibly and in line with God's will. The Bible is clear about giving the "first fruits" to the Lord, beginning with Genesis 14:20: *'And blessed be God Most High, who delivered your enemies into your hand.' Then Abram gave him a tenth of everything.* Giving 10 percent of your income may seem contrary to the concept of spending less, but it's a biblical pre-requisite to personal and financial health. Once we recognize that all provisions come from God and we are simply called to be good stewards of these gifts, the concept of giving a small percentage back to Him is too compelling to ignore. It's simple evidence that we recognize these material blessings as His provisions and that we're not placing our loyalties in them. As Richard Swenson so aptly wrote in his book, *Margin*, "money belongs to God, wealth belongs to God, the Kingdom belongs to God, we belong to God...only the choice belongs to us."[30]

- *Don't spend to your income.* How many times do we get an increase in income that immediately translates to a higher cost of living? Our increase in spending is sometimes even greater than our increase in income. We rationalize the need for more furniture, more activities for the kids, or new clothes. How closely do your family finances conform to the following model prescribed by Crown Financial Ministry?

Cost category	Percent of net, spendable income (After tax and tithing)
Home mortgage/rent	32 %
Car related expenses	13 %
Food	13 %
Insurance	5 %
Savings	5 %
Entertainment/vacation	6 %
Clothing	5 %
Med/Dental	4 %
School/Child care	5 %
Miscellaneous	7 %

- *Married couples—work as a team.* Talk about spending priorities, agree on a budget, and agree on giving and saving targets. Finances are among the biggest sources of conflict in many marriages. If a couple can't talk openly, honestly, and objectively about their finances, other elements of their marriage will be impacted: intimacy, their careers, and even the children's well-being.

- *Make hard decisions and establish spending disciplines.* It's obviously best if you never get into the overspending cycle, but even as habits have been formed, they too can be broken. Remember, Chapter 9 covers this topic in more depth.

- *Increase savings.* There's nothing as unsettling as not having a safety net for the future. We're all vulnerable to the unforeseen crisis—an illness, a layoff, or any other emergency. Most financial advisors recommend setting aside at least six months of expenses for crisis situations.

With your finances in order, you can focus on the steps to executing the rest of your plan.

What's needed to achieve your career vision and goal?

When you decide to pursue a new or even a slightly modified approach to your career path, it's important to identify the resources you'll need to get there. These generally fall into one of these few basic categories:

- *Training and personal development.* First identify the skills necessary to land work in this new field. You've already taken an inventory of your current skills, many of which should be applicable to this career, but there are likely others you'll require to obtain the job and, more importantly, to succeed. In some cases, this will require formal education at a college or university. Others will find that vocational schools offer a less expensive and more focused approach. Or you may simply require on-the-job training or an internship. One more important caveat: Just because you are certified for a specific career based on required courses you've completed, doesn't necessarily mean you have *all* the skills needed to succeed. Take someone who decides to become a home inspector, for example. Many who decide on careers like this have the knowledge for the trade itself but often lack the more intangible skills needed to be successful — like knowing how to market their business to real estate agents who frequently refer homebuyers to them. You could be the greatest inspector this side of the Mississippi, but if potential customers don't know how good you are, you'll be a hungry inspector. Examples of other "soft skills" that could be important include:

o   Time management
o   Project management
o   Financial acumen—budgeting, planning, etc.
o   Management—hiring, people development, etc.

Consult with others in your chosen line of work and ensure that you formulate a comprehensive personal development plan that outlines the skills you have today, the skills required to succeed for your career goal, and your plan to fill the gaps between the two.

• *Financial investment- in you!* In many cases you'll need to invest some money to get from where you are today to where you aspire to be. This money may pay for training, or you may need it to pay your monthly bills while you're being trained. Regardless, determine how you can fund your transition. Too many workers are stifled by their lack of financial resources to find a better way and yet, this may be the best investment any of us can make. It's better than most financial instruments because you're investing in the biggest cash-generating asset you own: you! Think about it—even if you have to spend $10,000 to invest in your next career, if that investment translates into your income-generating market value of an extra $5,000 per year, you're getting a 50 percent <u>annual</u> return on your investment. Where else can you get that? You have to think of this as investing in the Me, Inc. business. I'd much rather take a home equity loan to spend serious money on an investment in my skills or a new business than to remodel a kitchen. Only one of these options pays you back every year for the rest of your life—and it isn't the kitchen!

- *People resources.* You don't have to walk this journey alone. In fact, no one should. We all need help, and if that help comes from those who have more experience in your chosen field or have gone through a career transition themselves, all the better. You may need help from a variety of people. Some may help you navigate the training and education landscape. Others may help you to meet some good network contacts. Still others may allow you to intern in their business to help you learn a new trade. You'll be delighted and likely surprised by how willing the average person is to come alongside you in this exciting journey.

Document your plan and timeline

Now it's time to pull all of this together in a plan. This doesn't have to be a complicated document that you write and then never pick up again. Instead, create a summary of the timeline and key milestones for the journey. As you'll see in the template we've provided at <u>www.betterwayto-makealiving.com</u>, it should answer the following types of questions:

- What's my vision of success in this journey?
- How will I fund this transition? If necessary, will I use savings, debt (perhaps a home equity loan or low interest student loan), or something else?
- When will I start this process and how do I define progress?
- How and when will I transition from my current job/ career to the new? Will I need to do one full-time and the other part-time for some period?
- What are my risks and dependencies?

Create a "Board of Advisors"

There's strength in numbers, and it's always a good idea to surround yourself with wise counsel. Invite two to four people whom you know and trust—and who know you well enough to speak the truth in love—and ask them to be on your 'board of advisors.' This gives you an outlet to generate ideas and validate your plans and assumptions, and it creates a degree of accountability to sustain your momentum. I have friends who have actually formalized this process with meetings of their mentors/advisors, and it was of tremendous value to them (and to the advisors for that matter).

Share your plan with these trusted advisors and take advantage of their insights and perspectives. If they think you're being overly aggressive in your assumptions, take their input seriously. If they think you're not cut out for this plan and career, try to understand why. Ultimately, the decision to proceed is yours, but be careful not to ignore wise counsel.

Final Thoughts

The challenge and opportunity is compelling: If you're not satisfied in your current work and don't feel that you're doing what God meant for you to do, be bold and faithful. He designed you with a unique set of skills and attributes for a purpose. He is most glorified when you are using those skills. Put a plan together and then execute the plan. With a well-thought-out plan, you'll be energized by the entire process and the prospects for your future. Without one, you'll probably go nowhere fast. Your plan, along with faith that God will guide you, should give you confidence and the motivation to persist in making your plan a reality. Take the Morganstern's journey as an example:

~ Living life on God's terms: Bill Morganstern ~

Bill grew up in New Hampshire in a lower-middle-class family. An accomplished athlete and student leader in high school, he chose to attend the University of New Hampshire over his Ivy League options—partly because he found the environment more conducive to his desire to party. It would be the first of several decisions that eventually led to his alcoholism.

Armed with a degree in mechanical engineering, Bill started his career in sales training at Caterpillar Tractor Company, which ultimately led to other sales and management positions in the heavy equipment arena. Bill says of the early years of his career, "I found myself in lucrative and exciting positions with challenges, responsibility, and authority, but I couldn't ignore the feeling that I wasn't adding any lasting or really meaningful value to the world or to the people in it. The truth is, I spent a lot of time over several years trying to drown the uncomfortable feelings with alcohol."

After years of honing his management skills in the Northeast, he decided to look for another job and developed a plan. He was determined to live in Texas, even though he didn't know a single person there. He quit his job and began implementing his transition strategy. He remembers it well: "My friends and family thought

I had lost my mind. When I was leaving to fly to Texas to begin my networking process, my wife wondered how long I'd be gone, I replied with all sincerity, 'Until I find another job.'"

His strategy was successful—and, by his own admission, lucky. Within four weeks he had accepted a position as general manager of an equipment dealer making more than double the salary he had left behind. "The friends who previously thought I was crazy were now seeking my help for their career frustrations."

Although he was successful in the position, he still remembers having a hole in his gut (he calls it the "God Hole" now) because he was not adding intrinsic value to other people's lives. He tried to compensate for that by volunteering to counsel people in their own career search. That was the first indication of what he would ultimately determine to be his strength and calling in life.

Bill gave speeches about career transition at local colleges, earned his MBA from Pepperdine University on weekends and evenings, and even wrote his thesis paper for the MBA program on "Career Changes of Professionals Versus Their Job Satisfaction." He did all of this while still working as the general manager for the equipment company.

"It wasn't long before I came to realize that I loved my avocation—helping those in career transition—but was bored to death with my vocation and felt trapped by the golden handcuffs that come with financial success at an early age. Nevertheless, as my drinking and career dissatisfaction progressed, I knew I had to either do something or die a frustrated old man."

Bill was soon offered a position to open the Houston office of a startup outplacement firm. The good news: The challenge was exhilarating. The bad news: He would lose a company car and country club membership and have to take a $50,000 cut in annual salary—in 1980 dollars! Bill recalls, "After discussing the situation with my wife, Diane, and after much heart-wrenching prayer, we decided that we could make the sacrifices necessary to change our lifestyle to do what I really felt called to do." It turned out to be the right decision and 15 months later Bill started his own outplacement firm.

Bill would face another defining moment at that time. His dependence on alcohol was growing worse and the hole in his gut that he still didn't fully comprehend was growing larger. He eventually joined a 12-step program, and during his recovery he came to faith in Jesus Christ. "I gradually committed my all to him and began practicing biblical principles in all of my affairs, including my business. And the blessings haven't stopped—emotionally, financially, and, most importantly, spiritually."

Within a few short years, Bill was making more money than before and was infinitely happier, which, he says, "also confirmed my belief that financial success tends to take care of itself if your career choice is right."

Bill sold his business to a large outplacement firm in 2001 and still works almost exclusively with top-level executives in career transition who consistently struggle with life's purpose, balance, and spiritual issues.

"Since I started my own business in 1983, I was able to make a reasonable living, spend most of my time helping other people, and foster and strengthen my passion and relationship with Jesus Christ," Bill explained with a genuine sense of satisfaction. "Work was always the centerpiece of my life until I became sober. Work still occupied most of my time and effort until 1994. Since then, it's become more of a means to an end—the end being serving God."

When I asked him what he thought separated those who find work fulfilling and satisfying from those that don't, he thought for a minute and concluded, "Expectations. If a person's attitude is 'whatever God wants me to do is OK with me,' he will likely be eternally satisfied, even delighted by what life brings. The person whose self-determined expectations are high is likely to be disappointed."

Lessons Learned

Bill summarized a few important lessons, "Reduce expenses: Take fewer vacations, keep a car for ten years, understand the difference between needs and wants, and buy a smaller house. This is a key ingredient to providing the flexibility to change careers, try new things, and have balance in life." He added, "Put God at the center. I always said I'd commit time and effort to God when I retire. I learned that God wanted my heart and time sooner, not later, and he got my attention. And don't make the mistake of looking for the big thing God wants you to do someday. He wants us to simply be obedient, prayerful, and thirsty for His word. God will make sure you find your way."

Chapter 13 Reflection Questions:

- Have you developed a vision for the work that God has created you for and for you? Share it with a few people whose opinions you trust to help test your vision.
- What lifestyle adjustments are required to give you the best chance to pursue and achieve this vision? Reduce debt and expenses? Make time available by reducing other obligations?
- Have you developed a plan with specific action items and dates to establish objectives and track your progress?

Chapter 14

Persist: It Won't Happen By Accident

—◊◊◊—

As you get into "execution mode" in this journey, you'll find that it's both invigorating and intimidating at the same time. You're excited because you now have a vision of where you feel called to work and contribute, and that's exciting by itself. It's akin to the weeks before a vacation—we're fueled by the pleasant thoughts of what lies ahead and that anticipation keeps us motivated (at work and beyond). On the other hand, though deciding to change careers can give you a real sense of hope, the uncertainty of it can be intimidating. You'll have many questions and doubts in these uncharted waters: "How long will it take?" and "Will I be successful?" among many others. At this stage, *persistence* becomes a key factor in overcoming these daunting doubts.

Obedience

When God is tugging at you to follow His call and to use the gifts and talents He's given you, it's best to listen. In fact, it can become a matter of obedience.

Several months ago, I was having breakfast with Brian Ray, the founder of the Crossroads Career® Network and my partner in this ministry. He had invited another gentleman to join us who had expressed an interest in having his church enroll as a Crossroads member. I had never met this man before, and we had a nice cordial conversation about our ministry. Everything was going well until I happened to mention that I was in the process of writing this book. Our guest began to ask some questions — starting with the general ("What's the book about?") and getting increasingly pointed ("Do you feel called to write this book?" and "Why aren't you spending more time writing?"). He proceeded to spend the next 15 minutes challenging me as intensely as anyone has challenged me in my adult life about whether I am being obedient to God's call. My initial reaction to this confrontation was less than stellar. I felt very defensive, maybe even threatened.

Once I had a few minutes to process the discussion and separate my emotion from my brain, I concluded that he was absolutely right. In hindsight, the challenging questions were a divine gift to me. I've had the thoughts and perspectives on the topics in this book for many years and I've always rationalized not spending the time and energy to write it. "I'm too busy; I'll get to it next year," was my usual excuse. In reality, when we sense that God is calling us for a purpose, not pursuing the call is a form of disobedience – at least it was for me.

The same may apply to you if you're in a career that doesn't match your calling, your passions, and/or your priorities. We can think of every excuse possible to stay where we are. Sometimes we even start down a path toward something better, only to let distractions and impediments prevent us from taking the obedient steps toward our goals. Why wouldn't you use your God-given gifts and talents as He's called you to do?

All of this doesn't mean you should blindly dash out, quit your job and jump into the next great entrepreneurial idea. On the contrary, you should walk before you run. The last thing most of us can afford to do is dive into a new career only to find out later that it wasn't a good fit after all. When you take even small steps along this journey, you'll find that you learn, develop your skills, and are able to adjust your steps based on what you learn. You may even learn that your chosen path is not at all what you had hoped for. That's good news, because then you're one step closer to knowing where you do belong.

This does mean, however, that if you'll keep your eye on the vision and take proactive steps to get there, God will honor the journey because He's glorified in the process. He wants nothing more than for you to be in His will and using your talents.

That may mean that you first pursue a new direction part time, maybe even at night or on weekends. Or maybe you join an industry association that gives you more exposure to people in your target line of work so you can get a first-hand sense of the people and the environment you're headed toward. At least you'll be walking in the right direction.

Preparing for the impediments

There will be plenty of impediments to your progress in this journey, and the more you recognize and prepare for them, the better. Think of this as a marathon, not a sprint. If you get a cramp in the middle of the race, you don't drop out and give up. You walk for a few hundred yards and then start running again. If you get dehydrated, you take an extra drink at the next water station and get back in the race. The same holds true in finding a better way to make a living...and a life.

The best way to prepare yourself for these impediments is to recognize the most common ones and prepare to deal with them proactively:

- *Self-doubt*. Isn't this the story of our lives? Aren't most of us, in our hearts, worried about whether we're really capable of accomplishing our goals? And when these self-doubts creep in (or storm in), they usually hinder our progress. We learn to stop setting goals so we can feel better about not falling short of them. I think the psychologists call this avoidance behavior. Some of the most common questions we play in our mind are:
  o What if I'm not successful?
  o What if I don't like it?
  o What will other people think?

  These can be healthy questions at some point in the process, but when they become nagging self-doubts, they're counter-productive to your progress. When they creep into your psyche, you need to pause and remind yourself that you have spent the time to truly understand your purpose, your calling, and your priorities. View this as a mission—for God's sake and for your own sense of peace. Philippians 4:13 may help in this regard, *I can do everything through Him who gives me strength.*

- *A dwindling financial safety net.* If you decide to go back to school, start a new business, or become a free agent in your current line of work, you may get frustrated and stifled if your financial resources get thin. This is especially possible when the transition takes longer than planned or when your assumptions about your resources haven't been accurate. One last time—do your best to reduce your expenses to give yourself and your family the most flexibility to stay the course and persist. Cost reduction is the only sure way to make ends meet.

- *Time availability.* Have you noticed how easy it is for most of us to find distractions in our activities that are often less important or less strategic in the scheme of life? It's as though we just love the comfort of being busy regardless of what activities are consuming our time. "Life comes at you fast," as a popular TV commercial says. The most effective and efficient people I know are masters of resisting this activity trap. Instead of reacting to life, they are intentional. They choose to spend the right amount of time on pre-defined priorities. Are you spending too much time on lesser priorities? Resist the argument that you have no choice about how to spend your time. You have as much choice about where you spend your time as you do about where to spend your money — perhaps more. Invest your precious time in exploring your future career opportunities!

- *The opinions of others.* If you're afraid of what others will think, the answer is not to ignore everyone's opinion about what you're doing and how you're doing it. Instead, distinguish who in your circle of friends and advisors are the most qualified to give you honest and objective advice. Whoever those people are, surround yourself with them, invite their insights, and heed their advice. Ultimately it's your call on how to proceed, but seeking and gaining their insights is critical. You're likely to encounter at least a few people whose purpose is not entirely noble. They may enjoy seeing others fail, they may be uninformed about your plans and priorities, or they may have some ulterior motive. Regardless, your job is to separate these "counselors" from the others and listen to those who are most qualified and trusted to give you advice.

- *Going without God.* Whatever you choose to pursue, offer your efforts and your career choices to God. He wants to be your guide in this journey, and He's responsible for the outcomes anyway. Early in my career, I would have pep talks with myself about a project or new sales opportunity. I'd recite encouraging "scripts" to convince myself I was capable of making the deal happen. I thought and acted as though I was in control and could make anything happen if I put my mind to it. What I realize now, and pray that you recognize, is that God is in control. If we offer our desires and our lives obediently to Him, including our careers, he is faithful and will deliver us—both in our work and ultimately to our eternal home in heaven.

~ God is in control – leave the outcome to Him! ~

Chronicle your progress

When we attend a special event or visit a new place, we usually bring along a digital camera or video recorder to capture the sights we've seen and the fun we've experienced in the process. The career journey is similar in that we all benefit by chronicling our progress. Chapter 13 highlighted the importance of documenting your plan – the logical extension is to update that plan (timeline, goals, etc.). For some, keeping a journal of your progress works best for you. Regardless of the format, tracking what you've accomplished and what you've learned can be helpful in several ways.

Sometimes looking back is the best way to see your forward progress. On a long car trip, for example, it can be very discouraging to focus on the six hours remaining in a 15-hour ride instead of focusing on the nine hours you've already traveled. The same holds true in your career journey.

Developing a written plan for your transition and establishing some milestones associated with the plan allows you to then measure your achievements relative to this plan and helps to hold you accountable in order to sustain your momentum. This also allows you to make adjustments to your plan and timeline based on what you accomplish and learn in the process. Share your progress against the plan with your trusted advisors to get their feedback and to solicit new ideas and approaches they may have. These advisors will be far better equipped to help if you've taken the time and energy to organize your thoughts and define your issues/questions instead of "winging" it.

Final thought

Know that that there will be impediments but take pride in your progress and continue to persist. It's part of the reason God created work in the first place—to help us learn, allow us to fail occasionally, strengthen us to overcome challenges, and most importantly, enable us to bring glory to Him. When we do so, we can also anticipate experiencing God's promise of peace, which is the focus of the final chapter.

~ There is joy in our work: Duane and Tricia Moyer ~

Duane and Tricia Moyer met at work—at a McDonald's franchise in northern California during high school.

Then Tricia went south for a sociology degree at UCLA, while Duane earned a business degree at Taylor University in Indiana. After graduating, Duane moved back to California and they married. Tricia worked as an executive assistant in the years before their twin boys were born (they now have three children). They had agreed from the start that they would learn to live on one salary and save the second income so that when they began having children, Tricia could stay at home with them full time.

Duane went to work for Hertz Corporation, earning three promotions in the four years he worked there. He loved the business but ultimately found himself in roles that were not a good fit for his skills. "I knew from the time I started my college career that I was wired to make a difference in God's kingdom," he recalls. "From the beginning I've had an appreciation for the importance of integrating my faith at work." And the role he found himself occupying wasn't the right fit.

After earning a graduate degree from Loyola Marymount University, Duane and Tricia went through an intensive workshop on life-work design led by Kevin and Kay Marie Brennfleck, authors of *Live Your Calling*. It was a seminal event for the Moyers, as it provided clarity about what they were made by God to do and how to leverage their gifts in the world of work. Over the next several years and career steps, Duane was learning, developing his skills and experience, and "making a difference" in a variety of roles:

•Led a youth entrepreneurial program for low income youth in NY City;

•Started a similar program in Northern California while also teaching in the local school system and developing a curriculum;

•Launched a Silicon Valley program called Faithworks that focused on helping Christian business leaders find "significance" along with "success" in their careers;

•And, joined a leading Christian radio ministry in 2001 in Santa Cruz that subsequently moved Duane and Tricia to the Atlanta area the next year.

With each progressive step, Duane was not only cultivating skills to succeed in his current role, but also learning new skills that would prepare him for subsequent positions. He learned how to lead people, to develop curriculum, to develop and manage a nonprofit organization and govern with a board of directors, and even how to raise the funds necessary to operate.

"God opens and closes doors for all of us," Duane says. "We've just got to be open and discerning enough to pursue the right doors to walk through."

Duane has always been the risk taker of the family while Tricia is the "voice of reason," and they've usually found a way to balance their strengths and perspectives. As Tricia says, "life is usually a bit of a roller coaster, but the ride has been a faith-building experience of learning to trust God—particularly when you see the markers along the way that have made it obvious that we are following His path."

The Moyer's have also learned to manage their costs during their journey. Nonprofit organizations usually provide modest incomes relative to most corporations. Duane and Tricia committed early in their marriage to pay off their student loans, to spend on needs vs. wants, and to drive "mature" cars.

Most recently, Duane has been a key executive in a fast-growth ministry called His Church at Work (www. hischurchatwork.org). Its mission is to grow the influence of the church through the work lives of people. "I'm addicted to my work." Duane says. "It's obvious to me that God has been shaping me for this assignment since I started my career. I have a genuine sense that we're making a difference in those we reach."

The Moyer's have been a great example of sticking with their priorities, particularly the priority of giving their family stability when it's most needed. They've had opportunities that could have compromised that stability but have resisted the temptation. Duane has also been a testament to the principle of constantly preparing for the next assignment through education, experience, prayer, and exploring opportunities as they present themselves.

Lessons Learned

Duane: "There is joy in our work when we have the right perspective about God's design for work in our lives. God has made my calling and purpose clear—and I pray that others will seek the same."

Tricia: "If you know where God is leading you, be committed and don't look back. There's no benefit to being uncertain and self-doubting."

Chapter 14 Reflection Questions:

- What are the key impediments to achieving your career goals and calling?
- How are you tracking your progress? Do you know someone who can help hold you accountable and encourage you to persevere?
- How is God integrated into your journey?

Chapter 15:

Peace: Getting It and Keeping It

—ຕ—

"I have told you these things, so that in me you may have peace. In this world you will have trouble. But take heart! I have overcome the world." (John 16:33)

Right about now you're saying to yourself, "So, what's the answer? Is there some secret code at the back of this book that gives me the key to a sense of peace in work and in life?" It's not quite that simple, but it's also not all that complicated.

First, here's what this sense of peace is not: It isn't a promotion with a bigger job title. It isn't making more money than you do today. In fact, I'd argue that you could have the job of your dreams and win $5 million in next month's lottery and still not feel this elusive peace. (Although I'm sure many would like to test that theory.)

Look again at the verse above—God doesn't promise us a rose garden here on earth. Instead, our sense of peace is based on things less "earthly." In the movie *City Slickers,* Curly, the crusty old cowboy, said the secret to life is just "one thing." But from observing many people and experiencing my own journey, I think Curly had it wrong. The secret to life actually rests in five things:

- Your faith in, and your relationship with Jesus Christ
- Your ability to be content
- Your "margin" in life
- Your relationships—marriage, family, and friendships
- Your use of your God-given talents — purposefully

Let's explore each of these briefly.

Your faith in, and your relationship with Jesus Christ

The phrase "Better Way to Make a Living" has been used throughout this book. There's one word in this phrase that warrants a closer look: the word is "way." God has made extensive use of this word throughout scripture, among the most famous of which is Jesus' proclamation in John 14:6, *"I am the way and the truth and the life. No one comes to the Father except through me."* God has designed a path for us to follow, and it leads to eternity with Him in Heaven. If our hope is in Him, we'll also have the opportunity to experience His peace (and love) while on earth.

If your hope and outlook on life today is focused toward and dependent on your current work and career, it's misplaced. Your only lasting hope is in God Himself. Jesus was clear about that in John 16:33: *"so that in me, you may have peace."* That means you need to know Him and abide in Him; and once you know Him, you'll learn to trust Him with your work and the rest of your life. Even the heavenly host in Luke 2:14 praised God in saying, *"Glory to God in the highest, and on earth peace to men on whom his favor rests."*

Trusting in Him will also virtually eliminate our tendency to worry – which is critical for a sense of peace in our temporal life. A passage in Matthew 6:31-34 sums up Jesus' perspective:

"So do not worry, saying, 'What shall we eat?' or 'What shall we drink?' or 'What shall we wear?' For the pagans run after all of these things, and your heavenly Father knows that you need them. But seek first his Kingdom and his righteousness, and all these things will be given to you as well. Therefore do not worry about tomorrow, for tomorrow will worry about itself. Each day has enough trouble of its own."

Worry is diametrically opposed to faith. Without faith, we worry. Either faith or worry will fill your heart and mind – which will it be for you? How much do you trust that God is in control, regardless of your circumstances?

Our "job" here on earth is to seek His will and better understand our purpose from His perspective, not just from our often self-centered perspective. To do that, however, requires an investment on our part—an eternal investment of our time and energy. If, for example, you were intent on forging a strong, new relationship with a person you've recently met, you'd have to spend both time and energy to nurture this relationship. It's the same in our relationship with Jesus. It requires time every day to sit quietly in His presence to pray, to read, and to grasp His Word. It requires time and effort to know and love Him. In essence, this means putting God at the center of your work, your family, your relationships, and yes, your entire life. God then becomes pervasive for each of us.

There's also a strong relationship between our obedience to God's call and commandments and the degree to which we can rest in His peace. As John 14:21 explains, *"Whoever has my commands and obeys them, he is the one who loves me."* Obedience in God's terms is not that complicated: love God, love others, and be a faithful steward of His provisions (i.e., be generous with your time, talent, and treasure). At the risk of over-simplifying, doing "good" leads to doing well in God's economy.

Your ability to be content

It's always been curious to me that so many people who start a new job really enjoy their job for a short period of time but before too long they're frustrated with the work, their boss, or something job-related. Why do so few people seem truly content at work?

One reason is that our society tends to do everything possible to undermine our contentment through advertising, the media, and our school and work environments. We see what others have and we want it. We see the new "look" and want to duplicate it. This "compare" mentality usually makes us dissatisfied with what we have. We want more, and we want it now! It's the American way. We live in an age of envy. We used to want big-screen TVs and then flat screen TVs. Now it has to be HDTV. Why? So we can enhance our life?

Yet we all know people whose mindset is different. They aren't striving to achieve more; they're happy with what they've done. They aren't looking to acquire more; they're satisfied with what they already have. I even know some who are downright embarrassed about their possessions, particularly when they return from a mission trip where they've met underprivileged masses who own little or nothing.

Why are some people perfectly content in any work environment, while others are discontent in the exact same environments? What's the difference? It's you!

Just because a person is content by nature doesn't mean they won't proactively look for better career alternatives. But even as they do they tend to be more thankful for their current job and remain committed to do it well. In essence, they make the best of every situation they encounter.

There's a passage in 1 Timothy 6:6-8 that captures the value of contentment: *But Godliness with contentment is great gain. For we brought nothing into the world and we take nothing out of it. But if we have food and clothing, we will be content with that.*

As author J.I. Packer has emphasized, contentment is both commended and commanded by God. Contentment is essentially a matter of accepting from God's hand what He sends because we know He's good and therefore it is good. The more we choose contentment, the more God sets us free. The more He sets us free, the more we choose contentment. For an example of this principle, read about the apostle Paul and his writings in the New Testament. He may be the "poster child" for contentment, given the circumstances he endured.

Contentment comes down to a few basic tenants:

- To the greatest extent possible, divorce your thinking from society's and don't allow the affairs of others to influence your contentment. A large degree of any person's happiness rests in their ability to be content with what they have and not wish for what they don't have.
- We don't work for the primary purpose of acquiring new things. Our work is what we do to accomplish God's bigger purpose for our lives. In this context, work takes on a very different perspective.
- Decide how much "enough" for you is. A recent study asked people how much savings were necessary to live a comfortable retirement. Interestingly, people with $100,000 in savings said they needed $300,000. People with $500,000 said they needed $1 million. Not surprisingly, people with $1 million said it takes $2 million. And people with $2 million said $4 million would just about do it. It's never enough! But God's

promise of eternal life is more than enough, and you don't have to earn or save more money to achieve it. It's all temporary anyway!

- Instead of focusing on getting more, try giving more. "Remind" your money that you don't serve it; it serves your purpose – in Christ. Giving may be the surest way to break money's grip on you.
- Finally, accept from God's hand what He gives you. He will provide us all that we need, though perhaps not all that we want.

~ God will provide all that we need, though not all that we want ~

Your "margin" in life

We've spent plenty of time in this book discussing the merits and the strategies related to creating margin—the white space (consider the "margins" of a book for example) in our lives. The reason this is so critical to discovering God's peace is that the most valuable life experiences occur in the margins. That's where our relationships are nurtured; where our ability to grow in Christ occurs; where we can enjoy nature in all its glory; and where we are able to rest, both physically and mentally.

Without it, we run aimlessly through life with lots of activities but precious little purpose or peace. Challenge yourself and your family to resist the temptation to fill every moment of every day and strive to create balance and margin in your life.

Your relationships – marriage, family, and friendships

God has made us for relationships with Him and with others. The challenge in today's breakneck-paced world is to allocate enough time to foster these relationships. Without special, God-centered relationships, the average human being is destined to feel emptiness – I call it the God hole.

But it takes a real investment of time and energy to develop and nurture these special relationships. If you're married, no human relationship is more important than the one you have with your spouse. Have you noticed that strife in your marriage, even little skirmishes, have a way of unsettling the rest of your life? The only way to minimize this negative stream is to pour your time, your energy, and your love into your marriage.

The more you can surround yourself with other Christians, the more peace you'll tend to experience. "Doing life" with other believers is not only fun, it's necessary. Proverbs says, *He who walks with the wise grows wise, but a companion of fools suffers harm* (Proverbs 13:20). Nurture your relationships to allow for caring and accountability and give selflessly to show others the love of Christ. It truly is by giving in these relationships that we receive.

Your use of your God-given talents - purposefully

Those who seem to have a real sense of peace are also people who are convinced that what they're doing, their direction, and where they're spending their precious time takes great advantage of their God-given gifts and talents.

In Ecclesiastes 3:9, the question is posed, *What does the worker gain from his toil?* And the answer is delivered in verses 12-13, *I know there is nothing better for men than to be happy and do good while they live. That everyone may eat and drink and find satisfaction in all his toil- this is the gift of God.* This is God's design!

And whether in work or in our spare time, we were designed with specific spiritual and practical gifts that God intends for us to use in this life here on earth. For some, it may be serving. For others, it involves leading people. The purpose and gifts of many stay-at-home parents are centered on raising their children to be strong, productive adults who know and love the Lord. Yet others have a gift of earning lots of money to be able to give generously for Kingdom purposes. All of these "roles" are important and valuable in God's economy here on earth.

~ No one deserves sleepless Sunday nights! ~

In the introduction I mentioned that the people I most worry about are those who wake up every Monday morning (after a sleepless Sunday night) wondering why they're doing work that doesn't interest them, that seems to have no useful purpose to them, and, worse yet, seems to be their only option. I pray that if you are this person, that you have been served in this book and that you have hope for a great career and more importantly, that you have a deep sense of faith and hope that God is in control – and will care for you in any circumstance – both here and eternally.

Challenge yourself to find your purpose and your gifts, and take advantage of the limitless career opportunities that exist today. Don't be satisfied to live a life of quiet desperation. Be encouraged that there are better ways to make a living and, more importantly, a better life . . . in Christ. One of God's most exciting promises says, *Do not be anxious about anything, but in everything, by prayer and petition, with thanksgiving, present your requests to God. And the peace of God, which transcends all understanding, will guard your hearts and your minds in Christ Jesus.* (Philippians 4:6-7)

What constitutes success in this journey?

In most pursuits in life, we have a clear view of success. In sports, you either win or lose. In sales, you either close the sale or you don't. What does success look like in your work life? Is it: A big, important title? More money? A big house? Great vacations? Early retirement? Or is it closer to:

- Lives impacted?
- A happy marriage and well-adjusted children who know and love Jesus?
- Honor, integrity, and always doing the right things?
- Glorifying God in words and actions?
- Finding and growing your relationship with Jesus Christ?

Have you noticed anything different about people who seem to have a sense of peace in their work and in their life? Here are the attributes I've observed:

- Humble
- Servants
- Generous stewards
- Striving to learn
- Student of God's Word
- Selfless
- Obedient
- Contented
- And faithful — in trusting God and His will and His ways

A Closing Prayer

Lord, I pray that you will bless the person reading this book, that you will provide insight and energy to help them pursue you and your divine plan for their work and for their life. Jesus, we know that you want the best for us, and we pray that with every blessing you provide we may recognize you as the source and in turn use these blessings to glorify you. I pray also that you will show us your peace Lord

Jesus—and that we will help others to find your peace until we are reunited with you eternally.

~ Confirmation follows obedience: Mike and Elizabeth Murphy ~

They were both Texas natives who met at Texas A&M. Mike majored in industrial distribution and became a sales engineer at Johnson Controls, and Elizabeth majored in marketing and started in sales at Kodak. They began their careers in Houston in the early '80s and eventually married in 1984.

Elizabeth's success in sales led to leadership positions both at Kodak and a legal printing company over an eight-year period. Mike had also been successful in progressive positions with his company and was offered a promotion in 1990 that meant relocating to Raleigh, N.C. Though Elizabeth was reluctant to start over in a new city, the Murphy's decided to go. In retrospect, Elizabeth found that starting over—and relinquishing many of the things she cherished in her career—was instrumental in strengthening their marriage and provided the foundation to start their family with their first child the next year. She spent the next decade as a full-time mother as Mike's career continued to advance.

The Murphy's were later transferred to Cleveland, then Milwaukee; in fact, they moved three times in one year with two kids in tow, and eventually added two more children to the mix. Like many, Mike became overwhelmed with work. "I was traveling as much as 80 percent of the time, and it was tough on me and our family." To scale back his workload, he joined a small start-up company that promised equity—and wealth, which never came. So in 1999, when he was offered a position with a general contractor in Houston, Mike and

Elizabeth said "yes" and were excited to be going home to their Texas roots.

Two years into this career stop, Mike found that the company and the position were not a good fit for him and, for the first time in his career, quit his job without another one on the horizon. "It was a scary time and my confidence was shaken because I didn't know what God had in store for me," he says. "But I knew I needed to take a fresh look at how I'd been wired in order to find the right opportunity."

Mike ended up identifying several opportunities, one of which was as an associate pastor at the church they had previously attended in Milwaukee. Interestingly, the job he really wanted during this transition, but didn't get, was with Enron (which declared bankruptcy not too long afterwards)—God often works in mysterious ways. Both Mike and Elizabeth were convinced that there was no way they could consider the church position; Mike had no seminary training, the pay was not sufficient, Elizabeth would have to go back to work, and they loved being close to their families in Texas.

You can probably guess the outcome: "God changed both of our hearts and found small and often obvious ways to overcome every objection we raised. In fact, we both felt as though not accepting this calling would be an act of disobedience. We had to take a leap of faith that the confirmation of this decision would only come after we took the obedient steps."

Elizabeth's insight on their decision to move back to Wisconsin is enlightening. "The children's view of Mike's work and of work in general had become negative because they witnessed their father not enjoying the last few years of his corporate career. Since he took this position six years ago, they've witnessed a whole new perspective on Mike's joy in his work—and of work overall." And Mike has been pleasantly surprised by how well his corporate experience had prepared him for the role.

The Murphy's have clearly made sacrifices to take this route. Elizabeth has worked part time for most of the years since they returned to Wisconsin, and they've had to be modest in their spending. "I still get a pit in my stomach at times related to our finances," she says, "but every time that happens, I look backwards at how God has provided in tough and challenging times, and I rest in the comfort of knowing He's in control."

What does the future hold for the Murphy's? As Elizabeth says, "I pray that Mike and I will ultimately be in ministry together." His experience, coupled with her gift for writing and public speaking aimed at encouraging Christian women in their faith walk, should make for a great team.

Lessons Learned

Mike: "When we made tough career and family decisions, it had to be a 'we' decision. The heart change Elizabeth and I experienced in our last transition could only come from God and was enabled by our ability to communicate well together and being open to His calling."

Elizabeth: "Be passionate about whatever you do; be practical about your options; be prayerful; and don't be afraid to ask God the really hard questions and share your fears. It may be His way of drawing you closer to Him."

The Murphy's are a testament to the power and the peace that's available in our life journey, even during difficult challenges.

Chapter 15 Reflection Questions:

- How much peace do you feel in your life today? Why or why not?
- Why is the concept of contentment so critical to our sense of peace? What can you do to cultivate contentment in your life?
- What do you think are the key attributes of someone who's living a peace-filled work/life?
- What scriptural promises does God make to His believers about feeling a sense of peace on earth?

Acknowledgements

—◊◊◊—

I have been privileged, since 2003, to meet weekly with a group of men in Alpharetta, Ga. as part of a career ministry called Christ Centered Career Groups (C3G). We have prayed together, laughed together, cried together, and simply cared about each other in ways that men, at least on earth, rarely have an opportunity to do. I have been blessed to know each of you and you have taught me more than you can imagine about courage, diligence, and the power of Jesus Christ in our lives. I thank you all for sharing this journey with me and providing much of the insights and inspiration for this book.

I'm also deeply grateful to Brian and Kristy Ray, my brother and sister in Christ in the Crossroads Career® Network Ministry. Your dedication to serving others in this ministry has enabled tens of thousands of lives to be impacted – you are a blessing in my life and countless others.

Tell Me Your Story!

—ɱ—

Like most people, I am fascinated and encouraged by
hearing the stories of those who've transitioned from
work that was arduous, unfulfilling, or even exhausting to
work that leverages your God-given gifts and talents and
provides a reasonable balance in your life. We've created a
place for you to share your story at:
www.betterwaytomakealiving.com
I hope to share your journey with others who can gain
insights and muster the courage to find "a better way"

Appendix

—ɯ—

L isted below are some of the largest (and some not-so-large but intriguing nonetheless) job categories projected by the U.S Bureau of Labor Statistics in 2007. I've added some editorial comments in the right-most column. (Note: where the totals don't add up in each category: not all job sub-categories have been included here.)

Job Category	Calendar Yr 2014 # of positions	Education:	Commentary
Financial Specialists (finance, accounting, etc.)	3,000,000	College	For those who love working with numbers. Predictable and stable work.
Business Operations	4,000,000	Mix	Wide diversity of roles.
Computer Specialists	4,000,000	Mix	Tech wizards only need apply.
Architects/Drafters/ Engineers	2,800,000	College	Creative and technical combined.

Life & Physical Sciences	1,500,000	College	For those who have an aptitude for chemistry, biology, and related issues.
Community & Social Services • Counselor/ Soc. Serv. • Religious	2,800,000 2,200,000 600,000	Mix	Those with a heart to serve others. Note the mix of secular and faith-based.
Legal Professionals	1,400,000	College	For those who love to read, argue, and defend our rights.
Education overall • Post Secondary • Elementary & Secondary • Other Education	10,400,000 2,200,000 5,100,000 3,100,000	College	Roughly 7 percent of the U.S workforce is teaching today. Compensation improving; job prestige growing; key benefit: +/- 3 months paid vacation per year for many.
Art & Design	900,000	Mix	Nearly 1 million people are able to use their God-given talents as artists!
Entertainment & Performers	900,000	Mix	Anyone for Baseball? Dance? American Idol?
Media & Communications • Writers • Photographers	800,000 400,000 150,000	Mix	Current shortage. Only gifted communicators need apply.

Healthcare Practitioners • Registered Nurses • Health Technicians	8,600,000 3,100,000 3,100,000	Mix	Current shortage; Employee's market: location choice; overtime common.
Healthcare Support • Nursing Aids • Massage Therapists	4,700,000 2,800,000 119,000	Mix	More than 13 million workers (9 percent of total) in this and the above category in 2014!
Protective Services • Police • Fire • Private Investiga-tors • Animal Control • Security Guards • Life Guard/ Ski Patrol	3,600,000 1,350,000 360,000 50,000 17,000 1,150,000 136,000	High School	The dream job for many young people. Modest income; some dangerous occupations; typically rewarding with high job satisfaction.
Food Preparation & Serving • Waiter & Waitresses • Cooks & Food Prep • Rest. Cook	12,500,000 2,600,000 3,500,000 1,000,000	Mix	8 percent of the workforce supports our dine-out culture And it continues to grow!
Bldg Maintenance/ Cleaning	6,500,000	N/A	No risk of a downturn in this job category.

Personal Care & Service • Animal Trainers • Funeral Specialists • Personal Appearance (barber/ hairdressers) • Child Care • Recreation & Fitness	5,700,000 53,000 46,000 915,000 1,500,000 623,000	Mix	There's seemingly no limit to what the consumers will spend to take care of our pets, our cars, our children, and our appearance.
Sales and Sales Related • Retail Sales • Other Sales	16,800,000 9,400,000 5,800,000	Mix	Selling is among the largest (and earliest known) professions in history—and still growing!
Office Admin. and Support	25,300,000	Mix	Extensive automation will likely reduce the need for some office support—i.e. administrative assistants.
Farming, Fishing, & Forestry	1,000,000	Mix	Not a bad way to make a living!
Construction Trades	6,600,000	High School	U.S. building and infrastructure investments likely to keep this segment healthy.
Carpenters	1,500,000	High School	Good with your hands? Like to build things?
Hazardous Materials Removal	50,000	Mix	Just in case you like to walk on the dangerous side.

Installation, maintenance, repair	6,400,000	Mix	As technology advances, so does the support required.
Vehicle mechanics	2,000,000	High School + Trade	Cars/equipment aren't likely to go away either.
Musical Instrument Repair	6,000	High School	Just in case we missed someone completely in the other categories.
Production/ Manufacturing	10,500,000	Mix	No growth in this segment in the U.S.—much is being off-shored or outsourced.
Transportation/ Material movement • Air Transport • Bus Drivers • Rail • Water Transport	11,200,000 157,000 750,000 110,000 77,000	Mix	Choose your preferred mode of transportation— nearly 7 percent of our workforce employed here.

Government overall
• Federal (80 percent not located in Wash DC)
• State & Local
• Postal Service
• Armed Services
  o Full time
  o Reserve
	12,000,000
	2,000,000
	
	8,000,000
	600,000
	2,600,000
	1,400,000
	1,200,000
		Mix	They just want a few (million) good men and women! Highly secure positions and pensions far better than the commercial sector (3 times better on average).

Helpful Resources

—ɯ—

- *What Color is Your Parachute*: Author, Richard N. Bolles – classic job search book; millions of copies sold
- *48 Days to the Work You Love*: Author, Dan Miller – Sound job search strategies; solid Christian foundations
- *Live Your Calling*: Authors, Kevin and Kay Marie Brennfleck – strong Christian perspectives and focus on "calling"
- *Margin: Restoring Balance to Busy Lives*: Author, Dr. Richard Swenson – Dr Swenson (MD) compels the reader to get time and balance back in our lives
- *About My Father's Business*: Author, Regi Campbell – Helpful framework for fulfilling the Great Commission in our work and life in an unobtrusive way
- *The Seven Habits of Highly Effective People*: Author, Stephen Covey – Millions of copies sold to people who want to better manage their time, effort, and relationships – at work and beyond
- *The World is Flat*: Author, Thomas Friedman – Must-read on the global nature of our work and our economy, both today and in the future

- *What Business Should I Start?:* Author, Rhonda Abrams – Good primer on evaluating your entrepreneurial options
- *Halftime: Changing Your Game Plan From Success to Significance*: Author, Bob Buford – Excellent for middle-aged professionals struggling with work and significance (or lack thereof)
- Crossroads Career® Network:www.crossroadscareer.org - Website with Career tools and links (patrons of this book may use promotion code "betterway" to access the career explorer resources for free). Check out the Career Explorer's Guide (a six step guide to help you walk through a career transition).
- U.S. Dept of Labor—Occupational Outlook Handbook http://www.bls.gov/oco/ - to explore current and projected job growth categories and short descriptions
- *The Bible*: The roadmap to a better way to make a living...and a life...in Christ
- *The Purpose Driven Life*: Author, Rick Warren – perfect for those who wrestle with why God put you here on earth
- Career Direct—An effective assessment to provide clarity on your gifts and interests and the corresponding career opportunities – provided by Crown Financial Ministry: http://www.careerdirectonline.org/
- Crown Financial Ministry—www.crown.org – Tips and resources to manage your financial resources in a biblically sound way

I'd also love to have you join an on-going dialogue on these timely, career-related topics that are relevant to all of us. Please visit our website: www.betterwaytomakealiving. com to share your own work/life story and/or blog with us at www.75million.com

End Notes

—ᄶᄴᄿ—

[1] Daniel Pink, *Free Agent Nation*.

[2] Society of Human Resources Management (SHRM) 2004-2005 Workplace forecast: A Strategic Outlook.

[3] Congress' General Accounting Office report on Contingent workers, June 2000.

[4] The Economic Policy Institute.

[5] SHRM 2004-2005 Workplace Forecast: A Strategic Outlook.

[6] International Telework Association, http://www.telcoa. org/.

[7] A Harris Interactive Study estimates the number at 45 percent, although they add that only 20 percent of the workforce actually feels passionate about their jobs. Published by Career Vision/Ball Foundation 2005.

[8] CareerBuilder study, PR newswire, May 9, 2007.

[9] Lynn Franco of The Conference Board, press release Feb. 23, 2007.

[10] Why Employees Walk: 2005 Retention Initiatives Report, *The Hudson Employment Report*.

[11] U.S. Department of Labor, Bureau of Labor Statistics.

[12] MetLife study of employee benefits trends, 2003.

[13] News@Princeton, June 29, 2006, Eric Quinones.

[14] Russ Crosson, *A Life Well Spent* (Nashville, TN.: Thomas Nelson 1994), 15.

[15] Harris Interactive Survey, USA Today, May 23, 2005.

[16] ibid.

[17] CareerBuilder.com, Jan. 25, 2007, consumer employment survey conducted by Harris Interactive.

[18] ibid.

[19] 2007 Entrepreneur Magazine's, *eBay Start-up Guide.*

[20] Citizen-Times.com article published January 4, 2007 by columnist, Anita Bruzzese.

[21] Russ Crosson, *A Life Well Spent* (Nashville, TN.: Thomas Nelson 1994) p. 31.

[22] Rick Warren, *The Purpose Driven Life,* (Zondervan, 2002).

[23] Os Guiness, *The Call,* (W Publishing Group, 2003) 167.

[24] ibid.

[25] A number of good devotionals are in print, including Chris Tiegreen's *The One Year At His Feet Devotional* (Tyndale 2006) and *The One Year Walk With God Devotional.* (Tyndale 2004). You'll find a variety of devotional resources at www.devotionals.org.

[26] Breakthrough Performance Survey published on PR Web press release newswire, Jan. 11, 2007. www.learningforperformance.com.

[27] *Journal of Occupational and Environmental Medicine,* cited on www.management-issues.com, Jan. 15, 2007.

[28] If scrap booking is of interest, check out www.creative-memories.com for career opportunities with this Christ-centered business.

[29] Study conducted by Roper-ASW in 2002.

[30] Richard A. Swenson, *Margin, Restoring Balance to Busy Lives* (NavPress 2003).

LaVergne, TN USA
21 October 2010
201718LV00002B/2/P